"Sheree Richnow handles a sensitive and difficult phase of life with expertise and charm. She is an expert at getting rid of "stuff" during downsizing – without discarding memories. Her trained eye won't allow valuable antiques to be tossed out with the trash. Those wishing to declutter their lives should read this book before beginning the challenging journey."

Bruce E. Mowday

Some of the actual names, characters and locations depicted have
been changed to protect my client's privacy.

Produced in the United States of America.

SECOND EDITION: October 2018
Library of Congress Cataloging-in-Publication
Richnow, Sheree R.
It's JUSTUFF - The art of letting go

ISBN-13: 978-1983595233

CATEGORIES
  1. Memoir
  2. Self-help
  3. Home & Health

Cover design by Izaak A. Holsapple
Front cover photography reference 2018: Ball and chain
http://www.123rf.com/profile_gearstd'>gearstd?123RFStockPhoto</a>
Back cover photo by Paul Facenda

Dick, Our many imperfections are what makes us perfect.

It's

JUSTUFF

The art of letting go

Sheree Richnow

Sheree

FOR MY SON

This book is dedicated to my son, whose love, patience, confidence and support have made my life worth living.

MAKE IT COUNT!

MB

Table of Contents

INTRODUCTION 3

A personal history 9

My first organizing job 13

Kick start 17

A priceless discovery 25

More great finds 35

The Hoarder-Culturist & 43

The 30-year old ham 43

In my experience 49

Watch what you toss 59

Plenty to go around 65

Bitter medicine for shopaholics 75

The furry sandwich 89

Gold, guns & garbage 91

The truth about collectibles 105

You think you can do this? 111

5-Prong Evaluation Process & 113

22 Questions You Should Ask Yourself 113

Life goes on 125

In closing 127

SPECIAL THANKS 129

TESTIMONIALS 131

INTRODUCTION

This book has been written with consideration for the worst offenders of organizational disasters to well-meaning minimalists with a near hatred of excess. My clients are lovely men and women usually ranging from their early sixties into their late nineties. Each has his or her own history that determines how they perceive the sentimental and monetary value of their possessions. When it comes to the re-direction of their stuff, these notions can dramatically affect their ability to be objective. The real litmus test is the reality of true market value and what that means to family and friends. The trend today is leaning toward minimalism. Gen Xers and Millennials do not want to repeat their parents and grandparent's bad habits of collecting, hoarding and taking up valuable space in their homes. This is a hard reality we must all face when it's our time to move forward and leave the stuff of our lives behind.

The good news is that Baby Boomers sandwiched between both spectrums of aging parents and their own children have proactively been coming forward in search of solutions to some challenging and overwhelming circumstances. Gen Xers and Millennials are screaming in our ears, "We want access, not ownership! Thanks, but we don't want your stuff!" What exactly does "access not ownership" mean to this younger generation and why are they declining to accept responsibility for our stuff? Younger generations have been watching us.

They see how our accumulation of unnecessary collectibles, excessive clothing, battered and beaten antiques, and out-and-out trash, as an elephant on our back, and they are neither willing nor able to take on our baggage. To them, it's like a ball and chain around their neck.

My hope is that through this memoir of my career as a lifestyle transition strategist you will come to realize the reality of your own making. Join me on this journey through my work with some very special people who have helped me understand what it feels like to face the truth about the stuff we keep, and how it can prevent us from moving forward.

* * *

Back in mid-2005 I began testing the lifestyle transition startup concept. Originally, partnered with a reputable auction house, I launched a full-service business designed to usher people through the process of simplifying their lives. One of the core concepts behind the company was to intelligently and thoughtfully re-direct unwanted and unneeded personal property for sale, or donation to charity. Many of the resources and connections I refer to are relative to a specific geographic area however, similar businesses and charities likely exist in most cities and towns across America.

According to Webster's Dictionary the word "charity" means "love for one's fellow human beings" and "generosity toward the needy." Some people tend to refer to them as "the poor." In fact, many of the people we help are not chronically poor. Due to economic conditions, divorce, loss of work or other circumstances beyond their control, some people have simply had to start over and would not otherwise be categorized as being "poor."

When it comes to Webster's definition I am proud to say that my clients have exhibited extraordinary generosity toward those in need. They simply cannot stand to see perfectly good stuff go to waste and are willing to pass items on to those less fortunate. I often tell my clients that anyone can call the "junk monkeys" and have everything thrown into a dumpster, but it can take an educated eye to discern between real junk and items good enough to be sold or passed on to someone else. Even though many are tempted to take the easy way out and call for the dumpster, in their hearts they don't want to be wasteful.

As the completion of my degree in Organization Dynamics was coming to an end, one of my final courses was in Environmental Science. One of the most significant things I learned was that at the time Pennsylvania was the largest importer of other people's trash in the country. I was floored. Right then and there I committed myself and my business to keeping as much out of the dump as possible. As I formulated the standards for my company I held that notion near and dear to my heart. A major part of the service was to provide careful sifting through tons of personal property, thereby extracting anything that could be used or recycled, then ultimately redirecting it to people in need.

I invite you to walk with me through this entertaining and sometimes immensely challenging journey of my experiences as a lifestyle transition strategist.

I can tell you from experience that when it comes to categorizing what I do, there isn't an easy catch-all word. My company, and others similar to mine are still considered pioneers in the business of dealing with another people's stuff. We are transition experts whose jobs are to intelligently lighten the loads of those who have accumulated more than they can reasonably handle, and to aid them in simplifying their overall style of living.

Whether or not you are a hoarder, collector, want-to-be organized person or spouse of someone who cannot seem to throw anything away, I think you will enjoy reading an accounting of some actual real-life experiences. You may even learn a little about what you can do to prevent becoming a person of excess.

Toward the end of the book there is a chapter titled "My 5-Prong Evaluation Process and 22 Questions You Should Ask Yourself." These can serve as starting points for anyone interested in either processing his or her own home to ultimately hiring a professional to do the job. In reality, it may be harder than you think to face your secret clutter demons. Even those of you who are otherwise pretty well organized; mentally and physically capable, you may find the process more daunting than you ever could have imagined.

Perhaps the pristine main level of your home is a mere façade for the disastrous mess and embarrassing piles of junk lurking behind closed doors. Don't get a complex about it, just decide to be pro-active and get started dealing with the problem. I invite you to start here.

Enjoy the read...

It might just change the way you
think about your stuff.

A personal history

For a short time, back in the late fifties, my mother, older sister, younger brother and I lived in a quaint little motel next to a sewage plant in the outskirts of town. As a young child, I didn't realize we were considered poor, but living next to the sewage plant was probably a dead giveaway. It could be rather aromatic if the wind was blowing just the right way. Somehow, we survived that unique experience and went on to live in many beautiful homes in some very nice parts of town.

One of the greatest things about my mother was that no matter how little we had monetarily we were always clean, neatly dressed and loved. She did her best to impart in us a sense of dignity and a respect for what little we had. It was in the early days she taught us to take care of our things, to pick up after ourselves and to work hard. My mother was meticulous with our home and that gave us a level of appreciation for even the smallest of luxuries.

In the face of great trial and tribulation she taught the three of us some valuable lessons, but most of all she taught us to use common sense. Since then I have come to understand that common sense is an acquired mental ability that does not come naturally to many people. I am eternally grateful to my mother for who she is and how she raised us. Out of necessity we learned how to make the most out of virtually nothing.

By the time I reached the fifth grade, we had already moved four or five times. By then mother had remarried. My stepfather was the one who opened the door for us to a better life. He was a real estate broker who was also a custom home builder, and a house flipper on the side. It was largely due to his entrepreneurial spirit and influence that our family was able to enjoy some of the finer things life had to offer. We lived in a lovely home on a cul-de-sac, with a breezeway connected to a two-car garage. Our home was spacious, stylish and respectable.

My older sister, my younger brother and I used to play for hours on end exploring the neighborhood, getting wet and dirty in the creek while collecting crawdads and snakes. My mother was deathly afraid of snakes but that didn't deter my sister from showing off her daily catch. In those days we didn't have computers or any of the other distractions our kids have today, so we were dependent on our own creativity for entertainment. Imagine that!

Directly attributable to my mother's penchant for perfection was the vivid memory of the price of unmet obligations to housework, and the punishment due when it was too easily forgotten. I remember one particular occasion while making my way back home after spending an enjoyable Friday night sleepover with my best friend, when emanating from the house was the familiar nagging sound of the vacuum cleaner. Feelings of nausea welled up in me, I winced, paused for a moment then retreated back to my friend's house in hopes of temporary escape from what was destined to become a grueling day of housework.

My mother was vigilant about the condition of our home and in the event any one of the three of us failed to do his or her part, we all suffered the painful consequences. She would line us up and take inventory of exactly who had forgotten to clean the cat box or vacuum the floor. Of course, no one was willing to fess-up so, in a rather painful way she taught us the meaning of responsibility and accountability. The impression she left has never faded.

Today those who know my mother think she is a rock star. Now in her late 80s, she stands about five-foot-three, has a compact petite figure and a bust line I have envied my entire life.

When I started my business, Mom worked side-by-side with me on every job. My clients were astounded by this seemingly "little old lady," who was clearly 10 or 15 years older than they were and still able to perform this level of work. I bow to her strength, superior knowledge and intuition. She's a pretty incredible lady.

Without a shadow of a doubt I credit my mother for being the driving force behind the core of my success. She provided the foundation for nearly every victory in my life. She taught me to survive and to care about people and about quality. She taught me to take pride in how I look and how I conduct myself in public. Most of all she made me believe and trust in myself, and to be aware of insincere and dishonest people.

It is largely due to my upbringing that I understand what it's like to go without, and how much it means when someone else's generosity makes life a little sweeter.

If you were raised around a hoarder, chances are, you too might become one. On the other hand, if your mother or father were minimalists and you followed suit, you can thank them now!

My first organizing job

My earliest recollection of the first organizing job I performed was for my mother's friend Mary Jo's two daughters. Mary Jo was a fabulous seamstress who made gorgeous wedding gowns. Her two daughters were about the same ages as my sister and me.

One day when we were at their home visiting, Mary Jo and Mom were having one of their "adult conversations," so we were remanded to the girl's rooms to play. Now, in our household a messy room was absolute grounds for corporal punishment, so you can imagine my fright when I saw the ungodly condition of our friend's rooms. As the primary instigator, I suggested we play a clean-up game and I began picking things up and putting them away, all the while emulating my mother's notion of perfection and organization. A little while later we proudly emerged and announced victory over the clutter. Mary Jo and Mom responded optimistically and followed us to the back of the house for a look-see and shrieked with joy at the beautiful site before them. The girl's rooms were spotless and beautifully organized. Then, the unthinkable happened. They opened the closet doors and there, piled high, were the remnants of all the stuff we didn't have room for! I have to say, it wasn't a bad job, even for a ten-year-old. I was proud of what I had accomplished and little did

I know it would mark the beginning of my journey to creating a revolutionary new business concept that would become one of the most in-demand services of the 21st century.

It has been over 50 years since then, and while I have taken a few interesting detours, my ultimate destiny has not changed much. When I created the business plan for my company I thought carefully about some of the key challenges people were likely to face when making a life-changing transition and how I could be of help.

* * *

For about a year and a half I worked as the director of community relations for one of the largest providers of independent living, assisted living, and dementia care in the world. My position provided me the opportunity to meet with countless elderly people and their families. I listened carefully to the challenges they faced as they attempted to process the family home and move to a more supportive and convenient community. Before they could make that move they would have to deal with the challenges of dealing with a home packed to the gills with stuff. They were overwhelmed – virtually frozen in their tracks – and most of all, they were totally uncertain of how to proceed.

Some of these people had lived in the same homes for 30, 40 and sometimes 50 years and had the clutter to prove it. The children of these lovely people expressed being overwhelmed with the daunting task of deciding what to take, what would fit in the new apartment and what to do with all that remained. Most of the sons and daughters – Baby Boomers themselves, had full time jobs, families of their own, plenty of their own stuff and no free time in their busy schedules. It wasn't for a lack of compassion or desire for their loved one, but rather the reality of how much time and energy it would take to carefully process the family home. Finding time to take on the significant added responsibilities would be nearly impossible.

With each passing day and the addition of every new client, I have garnered a greater understanding of human nature. As consumers, we have become experts at turning inanimate objects in to priceless memories. In reality it is not so much the "stuff" we love, but what it represents in our minds and hearts. Most often it is about the people we associate with a particular item, and that can make it even harder to let go.

Kick start

One of my most memorable clients was a retired attorney and part-time real estate agent named Stan. As we were sitting at his kitchen table enjoying a brief lunch break together, I started to tell him about my idea to write this book. He became ecstatic and began asking more and more questions and encouraged me to start keeping a client journal so I could recant my experiences. I assured him I held in my memory the really outstanding stories and had kept some notes in my files. Honestly, I had yet to enter a single sentence on my computer. My client's enthusiasm and encouragement gave me the push I needed.

Stan and I had been working all morning on the third floor of his lovely townhome going through hundreds and hundreds of books he and his wife had collected. I am always fascinated to see what people read, so we embarked upon a conversation about our many shared interests. We talked about places we had both visited and quipped about some funny things that happened along the way. Stan, who I considered to be my intellectual superior, was careful not to offend, even if I was not privy to a particular author or historical event.

A man in his sixties, Stan was a vibrant Jewish man with a slender build, slightly receding hairline and a full, neatly trimmed snow-white beard. His wife, who was recently deceased had been a prolific reader and was fluent in the Spanish language. Stan shared with me that the two of them had traveled extensively throughout the world, enjoyed many common interests, and successfully co-parented their blended families.

Shelf after shelf of books revealed a wide variety of interests, each leading to a new and stimulating conversation. I found Stan to be intelligent and sensitive, well-read and amiable. I especially enjoyed spending quality one-on-one time with him throughout the entire process.

One of the most difficult things for book lovers to do is to cull out their libraries. I know this because I used to be one of them. Not that I don't still love books, I do. Now after reading a book, instead of keeping it, I don't hesitate to pass it on to someone else to enjoy. In part, my job is to help people let go of things they no longer need or want. For a book lover, this can be a particularly challenging task.

As Stan carefully wiped the dust from the edges of the books and placed them in boxes for short-term storage, I chattered away often forgetting the dusting part. It's unlike me to overlook such an important thing as dusting as I go, but I knew my inaction was helping to make a point about how long the books had been sitting on the shelves...unread.

I didn't mean to lead you astray making you think Stan was actually getting rid of his books! According to him they had already been reviewed and culled out thereby retaining only those of continued interest.

It wasn't long before we hit another wall of shelves crammed with homemade VHS tapes of movies from the 40s and 50s. I jokingly commented that VHS tapes were nearing the same infamous destiny as eight-track tapes. Not surprisingly though, Stan held on to the VHS tapes too – just in case he wanted to watch one in the future. I smiled and told him I understood and let him keep as many as he wanted. I've learned to pick my battles. For Stan, getting rid of the VHS tapes and cassettes would have to wait for another day.

As we progressed through the house, we began working on the basement. We could barely walk around the perimeter without stepping over or around boxes, bags and piles of papers in need of shredding. To his credit Stan was a committed recycler, but remaining stacks of corrugated boxes and paper bags stubbornly impeded our passage. In a townhome without a garage such as Stan's, the temptation was to lug the recycling to the basement until he had enough to justify a trip to the recycling dumpsters that were a quarter mile away in the complex, making it especially difficult to consistently do the right thing. Sometimes the path to responsible recycling is often blocked by the means to effectively and efficiently get the recycling to its proper place.

When the project was complete, Stan was free of unnecessary excess. He felt liberated from the bonds of stuff he no longer needed in his life. Now...he could move on.

Books, and what they say about us.

Perhaps what we read reveals more about us than we'd like to admit. By letting go of our books we're seemingly letting go of a part of ourselves.

How is it that books can sit dutifully on our bookcases for years without so much as a peek at the pages, yet we still can't bear to let them go?

Too close to home

Back in November 2004 I made a trip back to Texas to visit my father and realized it wouldn't be long before he would need help. He was exhibiting some signs of dementia and was having trouble finding his way around town while driving. During my visit, we nearly got into an accident coming home from the airport. At the time, he was fairly sharp and had been living alone and taking care of himself for many years. He and my mother had been divorced since I was five years old and any marital obligation on her part to care for him had long since passed.

The year following my visit I received a phone call from my father's physician. At the time, my dad was 75 years old and had gone to the VA Hospital for his second hip replacement. His doctor told me there was no way my father could continue to live on his own and asked what my siblings and I could do to help him.

Within the week, my mother, brother, my son and I flew to Texas to help my father transition back east to live with us. After a visit to the hospital to see Dad, we commenced to take action toward the first trial run of what would eventually represent the epitome of the services offered by my company.

Moving swiftly and efficiently, we calculated all of the work necessary to prepare his home for sale. We extracted what was necessary for him to retain and then proceeded to sort items for a garage sale along with donations to local charities. This part was particularly difficult because I had not lived in Texas for a number of years and didn't have the necessary community connections to redistribute items to known local charitable organizations. Besides, we had a greater challenge before us. Before the home could be sold we had to completely re-paint, re-carpet, buy and install new appliances, upgrade the electrical systems and renovate the kitchen. We had 10 days – and we would have to do all of the work ourselves.

My role in the family had always been that of mediator and I like to think I was a pretty good one. However, anyone who has ever gone through a wedding, death, birth of a child or any other stressful event knows what I mean when I tell you that PEOPLE GET CRAZY! Even people who are normally sane can be stressed to the max and go really nuts.

About day seven we were trying desperately to hold everything together and get the job done as quickly and efficiently as possible. It was expensive, tiring, uncomfortable, and with it came the highest levels of stress we could have possibly imagined. Sleeping on lousy air beds we bought at Wal-Mart, we worked from dawn until the wee hours of the morning. Our bodies were bruised and battered and our positive spirits quickly waned. My son, who at the time was ten years old, had been promised a trip to Astroworld and was losing patience. It was intended to be his reward for coming along and helping us with the project. Needless to say, we never made it. We were a total wreck!

Eventually we completed the job and prepared to fly Dad back home to live with my son and me. We loaded the back of his little white pick-up to the max and my brother headed northeast through Louisiana just as Hurricane Katrina was about to make landfall. My mother, father, son and I barely made it on the plane before Katrina hit Texas.

Ironically, my business was set to open September 1st that year and I had just experienced, first-hand, an extreme example of what my clients might be faced with in a similar situation. I knew then, that if I could live through that personal experience then it was possible to help others navigate their own set of challenges.

The truth was, it was more difficult than we could have possibly imagined. The work was demanding, exhausting and messy, and those were just the physical aspects. Mentally we started out strong and optimistic, but it wasn't long before we were on each other's nerves. I learned that it is a very different experience when it is your own family than when you're providing the same services for someone else.

Under no circumstances should the potential stress factor be underestimated.

***Just when you least expect – everything
can change.***

*One thing is for certain...change is inevitable.
Sometimes you're prepared – and sometimes you're
taken completely by surprise. It's virtually impossible
to anticipate all of the challenges coming your way,
but many of life's passages are indeed predictable.*

*When the passing of a loved one, a divorce or some
other life-altering challenge occurs, you don't have
to go through it alone.*

*Whether you have family and friends close by, or you
consult with a professional – there's a wealth of
information and support available.*

*Don't go through it alone...
and don't be afraid to ask for help.*

A priceless discovery

Seeptember 17, 2010. It was a sweltering July day when my crew and I arrived at our client's home in Chester Springs. We had been processing the multi-million-dollar estate for a couple of months and were getting close to completing the project. My son happened to be working with me in the attic that day while two of my crew were down below in the garage.

Cleaning out yet another attic space is always a dirty job, but as usual I made my way up the ladder and began the process of sorting and handing things down to the crew.

My policy has always been that I am the first person in any room or space. I touch virtually everything that crosses my path, then evaluate whether it should be sold, donated or thrown away.

For the most part, in this attic were stored numerous antique farm implements, which for the benefit of the family's private foundation had been tagged, inventoried and valued by an auction house. As I handed each item down I directed the crew as to where it should go; this one to auction, that one to be donated, and other items destined for the dumpster.

As I worked my way around the attic space I came upon a rather large ordinary cardboard box loosely tied shut with a piece of twine. On the top of the box was simply scribbled the word "Flags". At the time, I didn't think much about it and at a glance assumed they were the probably the flags or sails for one of the boats sitting in the barn. They would require closer evaluation so the guys placed them in the back of my car. Once back at the office I removed the items from the box and could see they were more than just flags belonging to an ordinary boat.

There were six flags in all and I saw that four of them bore the name *Constitution.* Due to their sheer size, it was virtually impossible to spread them out on the floor of my large conference room, but my bookkeeper and I did our best to get a better look. I instantly realized the possibility that these might be of some importance, and on my client's behalf, set my sights on researching them for provenance, authenticity, and potential value.

From then on, day after day, night after sleepless night I searched the Internet for information on flags; *The USS Constitution;* battles from the War of 1812, anything I could think of to help guide my research. The word "flag" quickly evolved to "ensign." I learned about the original six ships built by the American Navy back in the late 1700s, and the purpose of ensigns aboard these fine ships. History instantly came alive for me as I entrenched myself in my research. I suddenly wished I had paid more attention in history class.

My first inclination was to contact the USS Constitution Museum in Boston, Massachusetts, so I emailed an inquiry to their research department. I was cautiously vague about my inquiry but needed to get an idea of whether or not they already possessed any of the early ensigns from the famous ship. The researcher promptly sent me back an email saying they did not have any of the early ensigns in their collection, which was in part due to their rarity and extraordinary size. They noted that most naval ensigns had taken such a beating at sea that they rarely survived intact.

Curiosity got the best of me, so I inquired as to their possible value and historical importance. At this point in time I had not revealed to anyone what I had found. I realized if they were actually the battle flags from the USS Constitution, they would be monumentally valuable to my client and deserved special handling and consideration. But, before I shared my discovery I wanted to be absolutely sure of what I had found.

I don't claim to be a Vexillologist, (a fancy name for a flag expert), so I proceeded to educate myself and to officially have the flags authenticated by someone more qualified than me. Disclosing my find to anyone at this stage of the game would require great discretion, as protecting my client's interests was paramount.

For quite some time Sam Freeman, son of Samuel M. "Beau" Freeman II of Freeman's Auctioneers and Appraisers had been introducing me to people he felt I should know and was actually responsible for the connection that ultimately led to my assignment with this particular client.

It is important to note that Freeman's was established in Philadelphia in 1805 and was the very first auction house in the United States of America. They have earned a stellar reputation, not just in America, but worldwide. It was largely due to their history and prominence that I considered them a prime candidate to market and auction the flags on my client's behalf.

When you deal in important antiques and collectibles the way prominent families do, you come to know a lot of key people in the business, as was the case with my client. The resources available vis-à-vis these relationships were truly significant and each bore its own role in the way the story unfolded over the course of the next couple of years.

While researching the *USS Constitution* flags I had discovered in the attic, I enlisted the assistance of Frederick Scott – a close friend, confidant, and luckily a history buff. Turns out he was the ideal research partner for the project. Every conversation, every spare moment, Fred and I dedicated to researching the battle ensigns. Between the two of us we spent countless hours toward our discovery of the role they played on the *USS Constitution* nearly 200 years earlier. We made a special trip to Boston and boarded *Old Ironsides* for a tour. It was amazing to stand on the actual ship where the flags had flown so long ago. History came alive as we began to understand that the collection was vitally important and the ensigns were truly a national treasure. *(For ease of reference, I will use the terms "flags" and "ensigns" interchangeably.)*

Faced with the important choice of who to choose as my resource for further evaluation and subsequent sale of the ensigns, I carefully considered my options. I looked to see who I felt was well-qualified and possessed sufficient market presence to handle the merchandise. I had come to know Sam Freeman as a knowledgeable and experienced professional with credible resources. Therefore, I decided Freeman's

Auctions and Appraisers would be best qualified to assess and auction the flags on my client's behalf.

With great faith in Sam's integrity and his ability to be candid with me, I asked him to come to my office. I told him I thought that I had something of interest. In the strictest confidence, I walked Sam through the research Fred and I had already done. A full three-inch binder held hundreds of pages of research we had collected over the course of several weeks. Thanks to the miracle of the internet Fred and I were able to conduct massive amounts of research in a short period of time.

Sam glanced over at me and inquisitively asked, "When did you have time to do all of this?" I replied, "As you can imagine, I haven't been getting a lot of sleep!" Before I could walk Sam all the way through my research he stopped me cold and said, "Okay, you don't have to go any further. I see what you've got here."

A few days before my meeting with Sam, Fred and I had dedicated an entire Sunday to laying out the ensigns and taking dozens of photographs. We measured each of them, wrote descriptions then carefully folded and stowed them in my large office safe. The next step was for Sam to take a disk of the photographs I had taken of the flags back to his office. The next morning Sam showed the pictures to his father, Beau. For the time being only the two of them would be allowed to see the photographs or even know the flags existed.

For many years the Freemans had been closely acquainted with an area military historian by the name of Colonel J. Craig Nannos. I agreed to allow Sam to contact Craig to discuss, in confidence, what I had found. Sam and Beau phoned Craig and before they could say much, Craig surprisingly remarked he was certain he had seen this same grouping of flags some 35 years prior. According to the records subsequently obtained, my client's father had purchased the flags back in the mid-1960s – which was synonymous with Craig's recollection. Unbelievably so, Craig knew what we had. It was a fortuitous connection for all.

A day later Craig came to my office to see the ensigns and discuss the next step. It took him less than a minute to validate their authenticity. I was ecstatic! We spoke about some of the options we could offer the client. Perhaps the family would choose to retain the flags, donate them to a museum or ultimately sell them. We spoke of their importance as a priceless national American treasure. Our hearts raced as we dared speculate about their historical and monetary value.

Craig and Sam suggested the reality of the market for such goods as being "very narrow." The sheer size of the flags would make them somewhat less attractive to most flag enthusiasts, as there would be obvious challenges to displaying them. Basically, the market would likely boil down to three or four private parties with both the interest and finances to afford the goods.

Great thought was given to how the sale of the flags might affect the client's estate, and once the client was made aware of the ensigns, he could opt to do one of the following: retain them, sell them, donate or perhaps assign them to another auction house. My chosen core group had already invested considerable time and resources and was prepared to request a formal appraisal of the collection. Once that was complete, I called my client and invited him to my office for a presentation of our findings where he could carefully explore his options. Everyone understood that prior to taking further action such a discovery would require careful consideration by the family.

The presentation went exceptionally well. My client was thrilled to hear the flags had been rediscovered and were in good hands. He recounted childhood memories of the flags and was impressed with the photographs and extensive research we had done on his behalf. After all, they had been missing for decades, once thought to be lost, sold, or even mistakenly thrown away. I was happy to know that my fascinating discovery turned out to be of great importance to the family.

It was nearly a year and a half later that the flags were finally commissioned for sale through Freeman's. Prior to that, months more research went in to authenticating the provenance of the flags and preserving them for the future. Freeman's took exceptional precautions handling and transporting the flags to numerous venues designed to pique the interest of potential buyers. They did a magnificent job.

To further add to the immense investment by Freeman's Auctions was a forty-six-page full-color catalogue. A true work of art in itself, the catalogue provided a thorough history of the flags, the USS Constitution "Old Ironsides" and the family who owned them.

Finally, on April 12, 2012, the main gallery at Freeman's Auctions filled with excited bidders and onlookers. You could cut the tension in the room with a knife. As my enthusiastic entourage and I sat in the audience, we watched and listened as the auctioneer began the bidding on the first flag. Bidders were not only in the gallery, but on the phone and internet. Each flag was auctioned off separately. We could hardly contain our excitement as the hammer went down on the last of the flags. The entire collection had sold for over $750,000. Wow! A jaw dropping three-quarters of a million dollars.

All were sold to private buyers, and to my knowledge none of the flags ultimately went to either the Constitution Museum in Boston, the Smithsonian, or any other historic institution. Again, the sheer size of the flags would have made them very challenging to display.

That day was the last time I would ever see the flags I had so carefully and intently focused on and protected for so long. Perhaps the new owners would find a creative way to display the beautiful flags or simply store them in a box for another 200 years. Needless-to-say, we were all very happy with the outcome and grateful to Freeman's Auctions for having done such a magnificent job for my client.

To this day, the flag collection reigns supreme as my single greatest and most fascinating discovery, one of which I am very proud.

Let go of the item…not the memory.

If you have a sentimental attachment to something but feel guilty letting it go – consider taking a picture and placing it on one of those digital frames.

Merely seeing the photograph on occasion will be enough to make you feel adequately connected to the memory it represents.

"Not only do I not remember what we got rid of, but I don't wish I had anything back! BRAVO!"

Kathy R.

More great finds

An important part of the services I provide is the responsibility I have to protect my client's interests. I assume nothing, including whether or not they are aware of what they have or what they know about the value of their property. Protecting clients from unknowingly disposing of something of potential value is a very big part of my job. As a good generalist, I know when to look closely at what I find and subsequently perform the research required to establish provenance and potential value prior to sale. Where and how the goods are sold or donated is contractually up to me. Clients trust my judgment and depend on me to select the best avenues for imminent redirection. In this particular case I understood the client felt that the majority of high-end valuables had already been noted and catalogued, and thus empowered me to be responsible for the balance of goods in the home - as well as to stage the property for sale.

An important note here – this was the same estate where I had discovered the flags. My client had already contacted a prominent auction house to inventory and tag all of the high-end valuables. This is a normal course of action, especially when the estate is sizeable and the collector is as renowned as was my client.

After the adult children earmarked items to be retained, I was hired to redirect all of the remaining property. For some reason, none of the items I'll refer to here had been previously accounted for by the auction house. They had simply been overlooked. Most likely it was due to the fact they were fairly well-hidden from casual view. Also, the attics were in quite a state of disarray, so it was not at all surprising some things might be missed. It took some serious digging in rather undesirable conditions to make these discoveries.

A tremendous number of items I extracted and sold on behalf of the estate were directed to Briggs Auctions in Garnet Valley, Pennsylvania. Briggs is one of the best all-around full-service auction houses in our area, and their ability to recognize quality and effectively sell product on behalf of their clients is truly one of their greatest strengths.

One of my favorite items from the client's estate was an antique carousel pig. Owner and auctioneer John Turner knew it was a pretty cool piece and in fact he happened to be acquainted with a potential collector of pigs. The poor old pig had a little bit of damage to one of the ears, and one foot was disconnected, hanging by a wire.

As with most Friday nights, I attended the auction. I was especially interested in seeing how much the pig would bring at sale. John began the bidding at $200; pushed to $700, $1000, then $1,500. Finally, the hammer went down at $2,600! Following the lively bidding process, the audience enthusiastically applauded. Who would have thought a pig would create so much excitement?

What's important to note is that this pig was made in France. Had it been American made, it would likely have brought closer to $10,000. Once again, my client was not surprised it did well, but had no idea it would bring such a great price. He was delighted with the outcome.

On three prior occasions since beginning work on the same estate, I had unearthed a Louis Vuitton suitcase, a beautiful hand-painted antique drum and a very old hooked rug. Consequently, all of my great finds in this house were found in attics. In this particular old Chester County farmhouse were three separate attics: one over the master bedroom, one over the old part of the house and another over the garage and barns. There may even have been more, but these were some of the specific areas I was responsible for processing.

The Louis Vuitton was found back behind a long row of very weathered old clothes hanging in the attic over the master suite. The attic was quite dirty and I was warned early on there might be bats, so my client urged me to be careful. I wasn't thrilled about the possibility of being dive bombed by bats, but I listened first and didn't hear any funny squeaking noises, figured the job still had to be done and forged ahead. Frankly, the thought of a bat encounter in an attic would be enough to keep most people away. Maybe I just got lucky.

The LV brand was not unfamiliar to me, not because I actually owned one or would ever be in a position of buying one for myself, but I am trained to easily discern valuable items from junk and am always in the process of educating myself. I know quality when I see it. In order to become an experienced personal property generalist, I've had to invest a good number of years educating myself about value and quality. Therefore, at a glance it is fairly easy for me to identify the ordinary versus the valuable. This learned skill is one of the key differences between an everyday organizer, a clean-out service or moving company, and the kind of services I provide.

In yet another attic over the old part of the house were remnants of childhoods gone by, old toys, games, clothing, some old chairs and such. Way back in a corner was a ratty old suitcase seemingly of no importance whatsoever. Since I take nothing at face value, I pried opened the suitcase to see a dusty, dirty old hooked rug with some moth damage and significant wear. I had the guys set it aside in what I commonly refer to as the "S-review" pile, and kept working. In the same attic in a sizeable cardboard box was a large beautiful hand-painted antique drum. When examined more closely I deduced it was either a marvelously preserved antique or an exceptional reproduction.

With those three rather interesting objects in my possession, I began researching my finds for the client. My dear friend and colleague, Malena Martinez of Malena's Boutique in West Chester has always been willing to share with me her incredible knowledge of all things vintage such as handbags, shoes, jewelry, clothing and accessories, so she was the ideal person to assist me in identifying the potential value of the Louis Vuitton valise.

What I didn't know at the time was the auction house had located, tagged and assessed 12 other LV pieces that had since either been removed from the house or placed in an "off limits" space. With Malena's help, we were able to value it at between $2,000 and $3,000.

The hooked rug was another story. It was a colorful rug divided in to eight different square panels and on one particular panel was depicted "Lady Liberty." Again, research ensued and when I felt satisfied my education on hooked rugs was sufficient I took it to the next level – to my textile expert. Her input provided me a basic guide as to its possible value. She noted the poor condition of the rug and said restoration would likely cost around $10,000. So, I asked the next logical question, "How much might it be worth once it's restored?" By her estimate, its value could be between $30,000 and $40,000.

Okay then. Now we're talking! Anyone who has been around this business for any length of time knows that as the seller, you never want to restore an item prior to selling it. The buyer always prefers to have it restored according to their own standards and budget. She offered to pay my client a mere $1,000, so I promptly thanked her for her input and kindly declined the offer.

To make a long story short, the rug was subsequently grossly undervalued by another auction house at only $800. The client gave the rug back to me to sell privately and I subsequently sold it for $2,500 to the very same textile expert who had previously offered $1,000. The risk of any future value would be dependent upon the quality of the restoration and the potential market for the piece once completed. Basically, she was willing to assume the risk for the restoration and potential upside to her investment.

My client had always been very specific about items he knew existed, but had not yet uncovered, so it wasn't unusual for him to provide me with a list of missing items. As with my other surprising finds; the Louis Vuitton, the drum and the hooked-rug; my client never made mention of them in the initial stages of the assignment. As far as I knew, he had no knowledge of their existence. He certainly did not mention the flags. There was no indication on the box or on the ensigns themselves that would have given me a reason to believe the previous auction house knew they were in the attic, or were part of their valuation and inventory process. Very simply, they were mistakenly overlooked. This is not an uncommon dynamic, especially in the case of a large estate where the adult children have not lived in the home for quite some time. There was no reason to believe they could have known about anything and everything that might possibly have existed.

Just a note of interest, the Louis Vuitton Bisten suitcase was ultimately retained by the family. I researched and identified the drum and learned the painted image was of Dutch Admiral Michel de Rutyer from the 17th Century. It was subsequently commissioned to another auction house where it sold for $1,400 – plus the buyer's premium.

A hard truth.

I have come to understand and accept the natural flow of life and of aging. The gray hair and wrinkles eventually overtake us all and the inevitability of our mortality edges ever-closer in our minds.

None of us gets out of here alive and we can't take any of our stuff with us when we go.

The Hoarder-Culturist &
The 30-year old ham

I There were dozens of outdated clothes from the 40s, 50s, 60s and 70s - more than two dozen boxes of liquor stashed under a bed and behind the Tiki Bar; at least 100 Franklin Mint collector plates; cash *and more* cash. In a way, it would not have surprised me to find the mummified body of an ex-husband, long ago forgotten, tucked under the bed for safe keeping. Needless to say, Mary's home was one of the most memorable hoarding cases of my career.

My crew and I had been sorting, marking, inventorying and taking items to auction and donation sites for a couple of weeks. My colleague, Malena, and her assistant made a personal trip to sort through all of the clothes, shoes, jewelry and accessories and she subsequently offered to purchase them for a considerable amount of money.

From the front door was a barely passable path that ran from the bottom of the stairs up to the second floor – which was also crammed full of stuff. Shortly after we first began the job, we discovered an upstairs bedroom we originally didn't know existed. The doorway was completely obstructed with clothing hanging from the door jambs. Layers upon layers of clothing shrouded the bed, dressers and floors. Even the bathtub was full – and not with bubbles and water. I couldn't figure out how in the world many of these items had even found their way upstairs, let alone in to the bathtub.

Except for the extra-large master bedroom closet bedroom number one was nearly complete. Clothing from as far back as the 40s hung haphazardly from every possible hook and rod. In bedroom number two were layers of unopened nylon stockings, literally hundreds of them protruding from dresser drawers and peeking out from under the beds. Style throwbacks from the 70s were obvious remnants of this former party girl's extravagant lifestyle. Lovely silk slips in every color, never worn, were stacked in drawers with tags still attached. Over 300 collector plates and boxes from the likes of The Franklin Mint and Bradford Exchange were piled like towers in corners all around the room. Christmas ornaments long forgotten were stuffed into closets, under beds and in every possible nook and cranny.

So far, I had discovered a couple of thousand dollars in cash. Paper money and coins ended up netting the client over $4,000 dollars plus $700 dollars in unused traveler's checks, jewelry and other valuables. It didn't take long to learn that Mary was in the habit of stashing paper money in envelopes and tucking them inside her drawers.

As an experienced transition expert, I have become very familiar with the idiosyncratic tendencies of the elderly. I have learned to thoroughly search from foundation to rafters until I am satisfied we have uncovered every possible, misplaced, forgotten, or hidden item. Many seniors who have lived in their homes for 40 or 50 years have long forgotten where they hid their valuables, so part of my responsibility is to protect my client's interests – leaving no stone unturned. I am always on the lookout for forgotten, unexpected and potentially valuable property.

I left my trusted crew to continue with the archeological dig in bedroom number two while I cracked the crust off bedroom number three. I always insist on being the first one in each room so I can identify the course of action then orient my crew and continue to supervise while I work and oversee progress in other areas of the home.

As I slipped on a fresh pair of non-latex gloves I shouted to the crew, "I'll take what's behind door number 3!" Everyone laughed. Only in my wildest dreams could I have guessed what I would find. With a giant contractor bag in hand I began peeling away layers of clothing from the doorway. I spied a beautiful powder blue dress from the 60s, I touched it and it literally pulverized in to thin air...bits and pieces floated delicately to the floor. Too bad, it was so pretty, and so were hundreds of other clothes we would eventually uncover during the eight weeks we spent at Mary's home.

We had come to love our client and we purposefully left her portrait hanging nearby as a constant reminder of the fascinating character behind the home. Buried underneath years of stuff was the story behind the lady herself. Mary was 85 years old. One of the most startling things I discovered was that she and I were born on the same day in October, exactly 33 years apart. We were kindred spirits in more ways than one, and that scared me.

Inklings of ending up like Mary in my 80s made me shudder at the thought. Understanding the inevitable result from years of collecting and the costs associated with hoarding and saving things became crystal clear. First-hand exposure to a variety of scenarios, some worse than Mary's, has provided me the opportunity to see how different my life could have turned out. It was both a little unsettling and scary to see how a person and her beloved home could become consumed with what appeared to be meaningless stuff and sheer excess.

As we excavated the final bedroom I discovered a box about 8" x 8"x 20". It was neatly buried under a deep pile of stuff. By now I was used to Mary's way of doing things, or so I thought. The box was very heavy, so I figured she had probably filled it full of coins.

Markings on the outside indicated it was a ham. Yes, a ham. No, it was not in a can. It was wrapped in its original muslin cloth cover with the label still intact. The ham was 30 years old! I gingerly poked my finger at the muslin and heard a strange and sickly crackling sound. It was petrified! I let out a hoot to the crew and they all came running to see the latest discovery. We quickly snapped a picture for the archives and I passed it off to a crew member to haul to the dumpster. In retrospect, I wish I had kept the ham to put in my "Other People's Stuff Hall of Fame Museum" and perhaps should have had it bronzed or something. I suppose the picture will have to suffice as evidence.

It became obvious from what we found in each of the bedrooms that our sweet little friend Mary had accumulated more than her fair share of stuff. She filled bedroom number three in the 70s; then moved to bedroom two in the 80s and finally to the master bedroom in the 90s. After all usable space was exhausted, she had to move out, because there was nowhere left in the house for her to sleep.

Then there was the upstairs bathroom – the only bathroom in the house. Normally people take baths in the bathroom, but not Mary. We could barely see it at all through the piles of clutter. There was just enough room to close the make-shift shutter doors and sit down – at your own risk I might add. The sinks were full; the cabinets bulged with stacks of linens, shampoos and bubble baths. It was packed full. It had become totally dangerous for her to navigate the pathways with her walker or cane. Since there were no bathrooms on the first floor she would have to ride a power chair up the staircase to use the facilities. Aside from being able to use the power chair I can only imagine her alternative.

More about Mary later.

Just like me.

In the homes of virtually every one of my clients is the revelation that we all bear something in common. The woman I was, am, and could have become is represented in the people I serve.

I realize that an unlimited bank account, access to too much credit, or an over-indulgent wealthy husband could have easily landed me in the same overwhelming position as some of those I've served.

In my experience

E very day in this business is a new experience. As this concept continues to gain more and more momentum and exposure, I enjoy providing a level of service that meets my client's needs and expectations.

Realtors, attorneys and financial advisors provide many referrals, but most of my business is a direct result of client recommendations. When you are good at what you do and they know you can be depended upon to get the job done right, they don't hesitate to call again when in need. I have come to understand the service we provide offers tremendous residual benefits. During the time I have been in business we have provided services to three generations of people within the same families. What a nice compliment – and an honor.

As people age, they invariably experience difficulty with health issues. They often become less agile, more prone to falls, they're disinterested in eating or engaging in social activities, and show all the signs of normal aging. With that process usually comes a "drawing within" or reduction in the size of one's physical and emotional world.

In the early stages of our lives we're in the process of growing and accumulating increasingly more and more of everything. To some, it's a kind of measuring stick of our success. Usually by the time we have reached our 40s we've accumulated most of what we need and want. By the time we hit our 50s we begin to re-evaluate who we are and what is truly meaningful in life, and for the next ten years or so we begin to re-think where we're headed. Looking around, we recognize this incredible accumulation of stuff that once upon a time made sense to possess. Now, we wonder...what's it all about? And, is it still a necessary part of our lifestyle?

As we age and progress through each phase, our lives tend to draw inward once again. We opt for smaller homes with living spaces conveniently located on one level. We reluctantly learn to let go of people and things we once held near and dear who have either moved on or passed away. In essence, our world begins to shrink.

Attached to these phases are the things that represent the stories of our lives, our interests, our loves, losses, hopes, dreams and frivolities. Having visual reminders within viewing distance also reminds us of our failures and often – our poor judgment. We reflect on our wastefulness and sometimes the silly or stupid things we insisted on having – and then realized how ridiculous it was for us to have wanted in the first place. We all do it. None of us is totally innocent. It's simply human nature – the course of life and learning.

When I take stock of my own life, the things I've chosen to surround myself with no longer seem to hold the same meaning. I've been through enough to know I can't turn all that stuff back into money. After all, things are only worth what someone else is willing to pay. It really doesn't matter how much it cost when it was new and hopefully it was worth the enjoyment it brought over time. Due to market conditions or even our distorted or uniformed preconceived notions of value, this can be a tough lesson for just about anyone.

Generally speaking, most people tend to confuse monetary value with sentimental value. Over and over I hear clients say they're willing to sell something *if* it will bring a lot of money, but if it won't, they would rather keep it in the family. This is tainted thinking. I tell my clients, "If it truly has a great sentimental value – then keep it." No amount of money will take the place of something near and dear to your heart. And, *if* it will bring a lot of money, and you're *willing* to sell it, apparently, it's not really all that sentimental.

The exception is in cases where selling off personal possessions is necessary for the settlement of an estate or for expenses incurred during the transition process. There are times when family members have difficulty deciding who should get what and what value should be placed on certain pieces. Regarding this particular challenge, I recommend a couple of options: (1) Each member takes an equal turn selecting from available items; (2) Take the items to auction or post them online and let them bid against prospective public buyers. In the event of a family dispute, the latter ensures complete fairness. In some cases, neither battling party ends up with the bounty, but the client or their estate benefits fairly from the proceeds from their own possessions.

Many of my clients who have lived in their homes for 30-or 40-years lament over how much they have accumulated. And, now that it's time to make a major lifestyle transition they realize their homes are heavy-laden with remnants from every stage of their lives – stuff they no longer want or need. For some more than others it is more difficult to let go in order to move forward. It's a painful reality often punctuated with the visual reminder of a ball and chain shackled to their ankles. It is holding them down and holding them back from moving forward toward a fresh new phase of life.

If I am able to help people change their paradigm about acquisition, use, values and re-distribution, I will have succeeded in teaching an important lesson on accumulation, gift-giving and the inevitable end to the lifecycle of every product and property that exists. It is a victory to be celebrated when we learn to keep all our stuff in the proper perspective. Serving and educating future generations about the inevitable dynamics of how accumulation, aging and lifestyle affect our choices is a personal goal of mine.

In the beginning stages of working with clients I've had the challenge of downsizing and coordinating a strategy in preparation for a couple's relocation from their family home to a retirement community. As their physical and mental health begins to decline I am called in to help with the transition to assisted living, skilled nursing and ultimately, one final move following their passing. I've had the privilege of coming to know and love many of my clients during their final years.

As I was formulating the idea of a mission statement for my company, I was challenged with simplifying the message. After all, I passionately and purposefully wanted to describe the full scope of my intent. It was particularly difficult with a business designed to be as multi-faceted as mine. It was like tying a lasso around the stars in the sky and herding them into a corral to be simultaneously tamed. Like many other mission statements, it seemed ever-changing. Tweaking a word here and there to avoid any possible redundancies, and trying desperately to be clear and concise without being too wordy were all part of the struggle of this seemingly simple task.

After weeks of solitary deliberation, I finally wrote a mission statement I felt would adequately describe the overarching intent and purpose of the company.

I established the acronym S.P.E.C.S. –

Standards for Providing Excellent Customer Service.

For the most part I'm not a huge fan of using acronyms because most are pretty obscure and don't really make sense to anyone but the company however, the connotation of "specs" or "specifications" was seemingly strong enough to carry the assumption of its meaning. Here's what it means:

S.P.E.C.S.

Standards for Providing Excellent Customer Service

To provide intelligent & thoughtful guidance; be sensitive to the client; show respect for the client's personal property & space; be honest & trustworthy; possess a high level of professional integrity; be socially & ecologically responsible; accept responsibility for our actions; provide added-value service by being informed & knowledgeable; and be a valuable resource to our clients & the community – AND ALWAYS OVER DELIVER!

My mission was amplified through my relationships with charitable organizations in and around the communities I served. I have often told people that we are the conduit from the "haves" to the "have-nots." In other words, I was perpetually in the mode of re-directing unwanted personal property from those who no longer needed, wanted nor had room for such – to people most in need. These were usually those who couldn't otherwise afford to purchase what they needed, and perhaps were people who had lost everything they owned due to fire, flood, or loss of employment. The reason was of no consequence. I merely wanted to ensure nothing went to waste.

While processing a client's home, my intention has always been to practice the following:

1. Thoughtfulness
2. Courage
3. Trustworthiness
4. Respect and honor
5. Clarity of intention
6. Human kindness
7. Loyalty to the client
8. Organization
9. Moderation – know when to stop acquiring things

Thoughtfulness, respect and *human kindness* are essential keys to working well with clients. There is no need for them to feel shame because of their plight, and no matter what, they deserve *respect* and *kindness.* I have often stood close-by reassuring an embarrassed and teary-eyed client that I had seen much worse. I truly believed that what they needed at that moment was encouragement far more than judgment. In most cases they were already embarrassed and self-conscious, and the last thing they needed was a perfect stranger making them feel like a lost cause.

Much of my energy is focused on helping people become *courageous* enough to let go of their stuff. It's not easy to face an overwhelming situation when you're wracked with guilt and shame. Let's face it, sometimes we all need help. From there, I ask a number of questions designed to assess their ability and receptivity to reasoning through their thought process. Do they have *clarity of mind?* Or, are they confused and tormented by what someone else will think or want? Once we move past the initial psychological and emotional issues we work in the areas of *moderation, planning* and *organization.* I explain how my ability to remain *impartial* and *loyal* throughout the process has enabled me to guide them in an intelligent and thoughtful manner.

All the while we're building an intense *trust factor,* thus paving the way for cooperation and a willingness to be guided toward their ultimate goal. Through the experience, the client unknowingly learns to be magnanimous. In other words, they have discovered how generous, forgiving and unselfish they can be. They survived their initial feelings of *humiliation* and emerged victoriously. Together the master and the student successfully conquer the old and embrace a new direction.

It has always been my intention to meet the client wherever they are in life. Sure, I have seen some unspeakable things and in fact hold the confidence of many of my client's secrets, but I always remember one thing...we are in this together. I am merely the one who has been sent to put an end to the chaos, thereby making their world a more beautiful and stress-free place. My reward is, in all cases, so much more than monetary. I hope to be remembered as a problem solver, a bit of a miracle worker, and as someone they learned from and trusted throughout the process.

It's a personal choice.

Which life experiences and familial expectations helped form your idea of things being orderly?

Whether meticulously neat or chronically messy – how you choose to keep your home is a personal choice. The notion of things being "messy" or "neat" is often based on your early childhood experience or spouse's influence.

Consider what happens when visitors stop by unannounced. Do you tend to act as though your home isn't usually a mess – when in actuality, it always looks that way?

Watch what you toss

Jim and Elaine, two of my favorite clients, experienced first-hand how the full array of lifestyle transition services could be a benefit to them. It was my job to process their home and then transition them to a local retirement community. My team and I worked together to prepare them for the move and get their home ready to turn over to the new owners. A welcome surprise was coming their way.

While excavating the attic, I came across a very large, extremely heavy lamp with a reticulated metal base and shade. It was so heavy I could barely lift it alone. Upon hauling it out of the attic I showed Elaine the lamp. She told me I could just throw it out or put it in the metal recycling pile. Neither was she emotionally invested in the lamp, nor did she care where it ended up. Being an optimistic treasure cultivator and with the ability to identify potentially valuable items that can be turned in to money, I opted to take a chance. However ugly, the lamp was an interesting piece and told her I wanted to take it to auction. She agreed to my suggestion, shrugged her shoulders and said I could do whatever I wanted with the lamp.

A few weeks later I received the auction settlement sheet. I phoned Elaine to tell her the news and she practically burst at the seams when I told her the lamp had sold at auction for

$2,000! We were both delighted and laughed about how an item perceived to be a worthless piece of junk could have ended up in the trash or recycling pile. The lamp was a perfect example of the kind of magic we make happen all the time.

When I first started this business I struggled with things like, what to do with wire hangers, how to handle the scrap metal, who would take the clothing, and where was the best place to take someone's old furniture? Over time, relationships with area auctions, businesses, charities and other suppliers were forged and developed. Contractors were tried-and-true or they were never again recommended.

Intelligent re-direction of personal property is probably one of the most important challenges we face. It literally takes years to develop solid working relationships with reputable companies and organizations. Once we gain an understanding of the best avenues for re-direction which is based upon categories and types of goods, we can deal with the logistics of disseminating the property efficiently and effectively. In some cases, it's not unusual to have an entire truckload of donations for a local charity such as GreenDrop, Salvation Army, Goodwill or Habitat for Humanity.

We stress the importance of being sensitive to each charitable organization's ability to handle the kind of volume we generate each year. We make every effort to let them know how much we appreciate their good work in the community and continue to supply them with respectable items of interest. No matter the charity, these are hard-working people who are in the business of providing previously used goods to the community at a very low cost. Keep in mind that some workers are really volunteers or low-paid employees who are not usually treated with respect. Always be gracious and kind.

Some well-meaning but unthinking donors pawn-off on the charity their worthless junk, atrocious, outdated, worn and stained clothing, when it should have been thrown in the trash. Recently reported on the radio, by a source I didn't catch, stated that only 20% of what is donated is actually re-sold in the stores. I presume the other 80% is shipped abroad to less fortunate countries.

Due to situations common to our business we are often in a position to clean out the homes of those recently deceased. These folks would occasionally leave behind prescription drugs and perfectly good medical equipment. Select organizations as well as the local police station and some small pharmacies, are able to accept and dispose of unused medications. One such organization in our area is CVIM, Community Volunteers in Medicine. Often times their patients can't afford the medications they need and CVIM is often able to help. For those who live in other areas of the country and would like to do the same, try contacting a local hospital for a recommendation to a similar organization. If you would rather dispose of the medications yourself, you might want to check the internet for some guidance. I understand from my resources that you can dissolve medications in a glass of water then pour it over used coffee grounds and then throw it away. You should never flush drugs down the toilet or drain, and putting them in the trash may be a dangerous invitation to someone filtering through your garbage can. The thought of all those drugs going in to the water system makes me more than a little nervous – and sick. You can also contact the DEA at www.dea.gov about the National Prescription Drug Take-Back Day in your area.

For a number of years my company provided household goods and furnishings to families living under the umbrella of the Domestic Violence Center of Chester County. The executive director, along with the rest of her angel cohort serve victims of physical and mental abuse. In some cases, they've had to flee their homes, children in tow, with not so much as a suitcase or toothbrush in hand. Not only was this course of action incredibly brave and courageous, but it was scary and often cost them all of their worldly possessions. What once seemed certain in their lives was cast to the wind in hopes of finding refuge and safety from a dangerous situation.

By being mindful of redirecting your unwanted personal property to charitable organizations you're helping others endure hardships you may never truly understand. I encourage everyone to help as best they can.

* * *

HOLIDAY HOUSE

In 2008 my staff and I created a special project we called "Holiday House." In the beginning of the year I shared my vision with our clients and they responded in mass by allowing us to donate massive amounts of their unwanted and unused belongings to the cause. New and unused items targeted for donation were entrusted to Richnow LifeStyle Transitions', Holiday House Gift Boutique, for distribution to people in our community. Holiday House was staged as a rather large and private boutique where primarily ladies and their children from DVCCC and other community organizations and churches could shop for the holidays.

Complete with refreshments, a gift-wrapping center, Christmas trees, decorations, holiday meals, gift cards and care for the kids while their mothers shopped, Holiday House allowed these families to enjoy holiday gift-giving completely free of cost.

Area businesses became involved by donating cash, services and additional items for the Holiday House silent auction where in our first year were able to raise money for DVCCC. This popular event was to be repeated annually as long as we were able to secure warehouse space to collect and store goods, then set up shop each year.

In 2008 we stuffed our 1,800 square-foot warehouse with beautiful gift items and dressed the space to resemble a lovely boutique. Over 250 adults and children shopped at Holiday House that first year, freely selecting whatever they wanted – all at no charge.

As my commitment to DVCCC grew, the community service arm of our company became every bit as important to us as our for-profit efforts. In years to come we grew Holiday House to provide for thousands of people from numerous charities throughout the communities we served.

Be a thoughtful giver.

Give often – and give generously. There are many people living without even so much as the basics. If what you no longer need or want can be used by someone else – please donate it!

By the way...if you want to donate clothes, please be sure they're clean and decent enough to wear. Throw away ragged and badly stained or torn items. No one wants them.

We donate some very nice things to charities and they don't need junk they'll have to throw away – disposal costs just add to their overhead.

Plenty to go around

In this "throw-away" society the tendency is to buy cheap products and when they break or stop functioning, we simply toss them out. Our ancestors thought more of their investment than to brazenly cast out a broken tool or piece of furniture. They valued their purchases, in part because they cared about craftsmanship and quality. With a little effort and some basic skills, an item could be repaired and re-used for years to come. As a result of our wasteful attitudes our dumps are exploding with trash.

It might sound funny but one of my favorite things to do is go to the dump. There is just something satisfying about being able to kick old, used and broken junk off the back of the truck. I enjoy doing so because I spend so much time meticulously making everything look picture-perfect, that it simply feels good to let go of real trash.

Even though the price for scrap metal is minimal these days, I contend that it's in the best interest of my clients, and the environment, if we collect the metals and turn them in for money. I usually call my metal recycling guy and have him haul it away, and then it doesn't end up in the dump. It's a smart way of dealing with disposable junk and unusable metals and our clients appreciate the extra effort taken on their behalf. Actually, we're doing for the client what they would if they had the time, energy, and a truck to haul the stuff away. There is a lot to be said for having someone else load, haul and dispose of the heavy junk that's been accumulated.

A good example of community in action was when I received a call from a church in Coatesville that desperately needed office furniture, supplies and other items to set up their new offices. They sent me an email wish list. When they first contacted me, we were not in possession of the things they requested. Ironically, just one week after the request was submitted, a representative from a political party in West Chester called and said she'd gotten my name from someone who said I might be able to help.

When the election was over they were left with an abundance of desks, chairs, file cabinets and other things they needed to get rid of – by the end of the day! My crew and I jumped into the truck and drove to their headquarters which was only a mile from my office. It just so happened we knew exactly where to take everything, and I sent the guys on their way to deliver the much-needed furniture to the church. They were ecstatic – what a blessing! We too were blessed in the process. It was rewarding to know we had been an effective conduit from someone who had – to someone in need.

Consider this common scenario: You have something to get rid of, let's say an entertainment center. You take a nice digital photo of it, write eloquently about how useful and attractive it is – you list it on eBay or Craig's List and wait patiently to snag a prospect. Then it happens. The listing expires and no one has placed a bid or called on the posting. You ponder your next move. So, you think, "I'll ask everyone I know if they'd like to have it FOR FREE! They just have to pick it up." Sounds fair, right? Then your son's buddy Joe and his wife express an interest in the piece and come by a couple of days later to take a look. "Hmmm," they say. "We'd love to have it, but we don't have any way to get it to our apartment. Give us a couple of days to see if we can figure out how to get it moved." Now you're pumped! Finally, you're getting rid of it and it's going to a good home. You won't have to throw it in the trash after all.

A week goes by and still there is no word from Joe. You've already left three messages. A few days later Joe's wife calls and sheepishly informs you they can't find anyone to help them move the unit. Seems no one is available to lend a hand.

Drat! Now what? "I tried selling it; even tried to give it away," you say. Then the wheels begin to turn, you glance anxiously into the garage where the sledge hammer beckons to you in a devilish growl.

"I'll take care of it! We can smash it into a million pieces and stuff it in the trash!"

Just then your wife taps you on the shoulder and says, "Honey, maybe we should just keep it. I hate to throw it out, after all, it's perfectly good. Can't we can make room for it in the basement? Hey, if nothing else, one of the kids might be able to use it someday." You reluctantly acquiesce and call your next-door neighbor to see if he'll help you lug it to the basement.

Not exactly the result you were hoping for, was it? It's not just the entertainment center, that's just one of many things you'd love to get rid of, but it never seems to work out like you planned. Your basement has become a dumping ground for all of the things you don't want, don't need and can't get rid of.

Hundreds of clients have told me virtually the same story. They're overwhelmed and tired of shuffling the stuff around. No matter how hard they try to do the right thing, it always seems to be a challenge, and that's why some people just give up even trying to do the right thing.

I can't begin to tell you how much stuff is out there sitting in basements, closets, attics, bedrooms, garages and storage units. It's not being used and people are desperate to know what to do with the things they don't want. Those of us who are blessed can bless others with the overflow of our abundance. If you don't know what to do with your excess stuff, please make it a point to contact some charitable organizations and companies in your community and take time to do the right thing. There's even a site called freecycle.com where you can advertise those items you can't sell or donate to a charity. You post the item for free and whomever wants it contacts you, then comes by and picks it up. Even if that doesn't work, at least you've tried. I will never understand people who thoughtlessly throw perfectly good things in the trash. Don't need it? Please...pass it on.

The real message here is there are so many ways people can help each other by donating unwanted personal property. Indeed, to do the right thing can be a real challenge. Fact is,

America is an abundant country filled to the brim with everything we need – and more. I'm convinced there is no reason for anyone in this great country to go without furnishings, clothing, food, shelter and the basic needs of life. There is PLENTY to go around. We can all be part of the solution – instead of the problem.

Holding on too tight

By far the dirtiest two places in most people's homes are the refrigerator and the utensil drawer. I know, it sounds creepy considering that's where we keep our food and the utensils we eat with. But, I assure you it is a frightening reality many people do not realize. You'll see what I mean...take a quick break, go to the kitchen and lift your silverware out of the slots. You might be surprised by how dirty it gets in there.

Let's look back to the story about Mary. I'm not easily surprised these days, but I have always been amazed at where people choose to store things. In Mary's case, one of the most unusual places she chose to stash obscure things was inside her dishwasher. We found food, napkins, paper bags, rubber bands, twisty ties and trash, but no dishes and no silverware. Mary couldn't have used her dishwasher for its intended purpose even if she wanted to.

The small drawer next to the dishwasher, normally used for hot pads and such was crammed so full we could barely pry it open. Every inch in every cupboard was stuffed with dishes, glasses, cookware, junk...and still more junk. Everything in the house had to be removed and either thrown out or set aside for donation or auction. I could not begin to count the number of contractors bags we used to extract all the trash. Then there was the nauseating smell I associate with finding a kitchen in that condition. It is truly indescribable.

When I can't quite figure out where the strange odor is coming from – I usually open the refrigerator. I look at the expiration dates on everything. If it has expired, I throw it out! Contracting food poisoning is not worth the cost of a $2.99 carton of eggs. I like to clean my refrigerator out at least three or four times a year. I throw away everything I don't want, need or plan to consume in the near future.

If you have children and perhaps a spouse in the house, you might want to excavate your refrigerator more often than that. They are especially famous for putting empty cartons, moldy jars and plastic bags back in the refrigerator. Better yet, assign the clean-out task to someone else and put her in charge of monitoring the cleanliness of the refrigerator. Maybe the experience will teach her a lifelong lesson she won't forget.

More about Mary...

Mary's home was a two-story Colonial with a swimming pool literally pried into a tiny back yard. As my crew and I worked our way through her home it became apparent that in her past life she had been a real live party girl. Mary's decked out Tiki bar was generously stocked with every type of hard liquor, aperitif and wine you could imagine. If I had to guess I would say there were almost 40 cases of alcohol, some dating as far back as the 50s – some aged to perfection and some disgustingly soured.

Mary and I needed to have a chat about the alcohol. Remember, she is 85 years old. I'm not sure how she made it this far without becoming an alcoholic and she tried to convince me that her party friends were the main consumers of her generous bounty. As she spoke lovingly about her days partying around the pool with her friends, I knew she was not about to completely give up her stash. I could see it in her eyes. A quick glance toward the Tiki bar would catapult her back to better times filled with laughter, dancing, and vibrant lively friends. I respected Mary's right to her memories and proceeded to make a list of her favorite libations, then boxed what she wanted and delivered them to her new home. She knew she would never drink it all, but for her it was a source of comfort, a connection to her lively and highly liberal past. I believed she had the right to preserve the memory.

What we know and our memories are the only things we get to take with us to our graves. All the stuff we've collected along the way simply serves as trappings to please our senses and make us more comfortable while we're here on Earth. We surround ourselves with worthless collectibles, precious antiques, sentimental letters, old greeting cards and special mementos that reflect our journey through life. It becomes more and more difficult to let go of reminders of where we have been and what we've done. Trouble is, some of those memories may no longer represent who we are in the present. It is our past, and we simply cannot let go. This is a serious dilemma for many people.

Ask yourself...

*What am I choosing to hold on to and why am I
so attached to my stuff?*

*If I decide to keep something, will it be used,
displayed, or worn by someone? Or, will it be packed
away for someone else to deal with someday?*

Be honest.

Give yourself permission to let things go.

Bitter medicine for shopaholics

In 2005 following the opening of my new business I was attending a private fund raiser for a major charity. It was there that I met a very special couple. To protect their identity, I will lovingly refer to my friends as Betty and Bob.

Dressed in their finest party attire Betty and Bob stood next to me having a glass of wine as we struck up a conversation. I was quite interested in the topic, as they talked excitedly about the possibility of needing my services. Bob went on to explain their overwhelming situation. Apparently, the basement of their home had suffered multiple flooding episodes that had likely ruined much of their personal property.

With a long-term goal of preparing their home for sale, Betty and Bob knew they needed to get help and wanted to get started working on their basement as soon as possible. We made an appointment for a consultation later that week. I arrived to find the main floor of their lovely ranch-style home well-decorated and tidy. There was some obvious clutter, but everything seemed to be in pretty good order. Betty's keen sense of style was apparent. Both she and Bob were in the insurance business and had accumulated some lovely things. We sat comfortably in the living room and I listened carefully to their challenges and goals.

As we talked, Betty and Bob warned me that what I was seeing upstairs was the antithesis of what I would see in the basement. Once shown around the main level we opened the door to the basement and descended the crowded staircase toward the foreboding abyss.

My preview to what was to come was countless shopping bags and a huge back-stock of jams and jellies lining the walls along the stairs, with mops, brooms and other assorted junk blocking the view. They were right, there was a tiny, barely passable path from the staircase to the garage door and then back to the washer and dryer. Bear in mind, their basement was a whopping 1,200 square feet.

I could not believe my eyes. I tried not to react to what I was seeing. Wall-to-wall and ceiling-to-floor, nearly every inch was covered with something. Clothes hung by the hundreds from rafters and make-shift clothes lines. Countless unopened packages lay stacked in mountainous heaps. I picked up a box, still wrapped in Christmas paper and asked Bob, "Do you know what's in here?" He put his hands in the air and gingerly replied, "I don't know what's in any of this stuff!"

We edged toward the garage door and he admitted to knowing there was a golf cart buried out there somewhere, but wasn't sure exactly where. We all giggled a little at the thought and I tried to make light of their situation. Now, any sane person might have seen this as an opportunity to take the path of least resistance and head toward the door, but not me! No way. I love a challenge, and besides, I needed the business. I would do whatever it would take to lighten the load for these lovely people. They were in clutter hell and it was my job to deliver them from their plight.

As we retreated upstairs to safer ground, Bob mustered up the courage to ask two key questions, "How long will it take to clean this up?" and "How much will it cost?" Since these were my early days in the business I was still learning the ropes. I was beside myself as I frantically searched for the right answers to his questions. There really wasn't a way to accurately predict how much time it would take, or how much it would cost, so I resorted to what has now become my mantra, "It takes as long as it takes." It didn't get this way overnight and it's going to take time to clean it up. As far as cost goes – I charge by the hour, by the person. We'll start with one dumpster and order additional units as needed." A week later two of us converged on the basement and embarked on a journey that would eventually take months to complete.

Together we proceeded to process Betty and Bob's basement handling bag after bag, box after box, hundreds of them, filled with brand new clothes, gifts and housewares. The quantity of stuff was truly inconceivable. After unwrapping countless gifts and shopping bags, we filled an entire dumpster with nothing but paper. I don't think the weight even registered at the dump. We brought in a half a dozen work tables, sorted and displayed everything we had unwrapped for our clients to review. Several tables were allocated for auctionable items, then four more for donations, and then of course, there were trash bags, dozens and dozens of them.

Since my policy is to intelligently redirect virtually anything that can be used by someone else, only real trash is thrown away or sent to recycling centers.

Upon returning home from work each day Betty would descend the staircase and make her selections. This was especially difficult because her taste was exquisite and there wasn't much in the way of worthless junk lying around. Much of what she had purchased or had been given hadn't been seen in years. Her ability to make decisions about what to retain for her gift closet at the new house was within reason. Impressed with her willingness to let go of anything she didn't really want, need or wish to gift or re-gift, I continued to encourage her to stay focused on the greater goal of downsizing and de-cluttering their remaining possessions.

Shock and amazement on our client's faces displayed both their hope and relief at the immense job we had taken on for them. All of us felt the weight lifting off their shoulders as we diligently worked our way through the mountains of clutter. Each day we would inventory, pack and load the truck with items destined for auction or charitable donation. At the time, since the business was still young, I didn't own a box truck, so we either loaded my Jeep with stuff or would rent a larger vehicle to haul things away.

At Betty and Bob's house we didn't find anything as scary as a 30-year-old ham in the basement, but we finally uncovered the old golf cart in the garage that in the beginning was not visible to the naked eye. It no longer ran, but we took it to auction anyway where it sold for $25. Loads of beautiful clothing, shoes, belts, ties, shirts, suits, purses and jewelry, some with the tags still attached, were taken to a local clothing consignment shop thus garnering a return of over $1,000 for my clients. Beginning with the basement and garage then moving upstairs through the kitchen, dining room, living room and back bedrooms, we not only downsized and de-cluttered the entire home, but subsequently staged it for sale.

Even though Betty had a beautifully decorated home there was still too much clutter on the main floor. I methodically worked my way through each room rearranging furniture and other items. By the time we were finished with the staging their home was truly a showplace. We were able to pre-pack many of the items they'd planned to move to their new home and then take them to a designated holding area downstairs.

Seven months from the time we initially started the project I received a lovely note from Betty that read, *"Sheree, thanks for all your hard work getting us ready to sell our home. We signed on with a realtor on Monday, had an open house a week later and it looks like we have a cash buyer ready to go! We couldn't have done it without you!"*

Throughout the duration of our job with Betty and Bob we received daily notes of thanks and optimism. They never failed to show their appreciation for our hard work and diligence. Never once did they complain about how much we were charging for our services. They were grateful for us – and us for them. It was a mutually rewarding relationship.

I will be especially thankful to these two wonderful people for their patience and willingness to allow us to touch their lives in a way no one else could. Their level of faith in my judgment gave me the opportunity to further formulate the processes and procedures I continue to implement today. Since they were some of my very first clients I was particularly grateful to have earned their confidence and trust. To this day, Betty and Bob are not only two of my favorite people, but by and large were the ones where I learned the most under fire and, was given the greatest amount of latitude to do what I do best.

* * *

Come to find out, both Betty, my other client, Mary and I were born a number of years apart – almost to the day. I saw some of myself in both of these lovely ladies. I came to realize the possibility that living a lifestyle where accumulating way more than I would ever need, and collecting a little bit of everything beautiful and pleasing to my eye, would eventually lead me to the same destiny. In a strange kind of way, I will forever be thankful to both of them. Because of them and hundreds of others I am not a hoarder or collector of stuff.

Do you know how to eat an elephant?

Simple.

One bite at a time.

Infomercial hell

Downsizing comes in many packages. At this moment in the world, we the people are experiencing one of the biggest downsizing trends of our time. For a while now, our society has been in acquisition mode, and its high time to re-think the way we live.

More, better, bigger, nicer...more, more, more!

As a result of this kind of thinking, our homes, attics, garages and storage units are loaded with stuff – stuff we don't need, don't want, can't use and can't afford to keep. Our cast-offs represent a penchant for our excessive appetites for consuming senseless and sometimes worthless products.

As a former advertising agency owner, my job was to entice consumers into buying the products my clients wanted to sell. Companies are constantly looking for opportunities to meet the needs of the consumer and to monitor and predict our future buying habits, so they spend an inordinate amount of time and money on research. Demographic and psychographic data are scoured for evidence that tells businesses who we are, what we want, what we like and how much we're willing to spend. They intimately understand what moves us. And with the power of the Internet the problem has become increasingly intense. Make no mistake. We can't hide. They know where to find us!

It's their job is to gather as much intelligence as possible and then tailor their products and services to obtain an increasingly larger share of our income. It's a noble goal, and in their opinion, justifiable. I contend it's highly self-serving and potentially detrimental to consumers.

I was reminded of that very point one night during a bout of insomnia when an infomercial came on at 3:05AM for a really cool abdominal contraption. Gee, how did they know I would be awake *and,* that I was concerned about my growing mid-life, mid-section? Further, how in the world did they know I would be willing to spend a couple of hundred dollars to have some machine do all the work for me? They must be psychic!

What really annoys me is that I spent 30 years in the advertising business and I know I am being manipulated. But, I'm smart. Instead of calling, because I know an operator from some foreign country is going to try and up-sell me five times, I pick up my trusty laptop and go to their website. After all, I want to be in control of my own buying experience. Or so I think.

There it is. I find what I am looking for and place my order; however, the computer will not let me go until it attempts to sell me a multitude of additional products designed to complement my original purchase. I begin mumbling under my breath as my finger hits the keys...click, click, click, CLICK! It's the sound of my banging away at the "NO" box. These crazy people just won't take "NO" for an answer. Drives me nuts! It makes me want to turn off the television when I can't sleep and go back to reading a good book. I know what they're up to but I can't get around the calculated manipulation, and it makes me sorry I bothered to order anything at all.

Perhaps some of you have shared the same kind of experience. In fact, I know many of my clients have because now they have to pay me to get rid of all those ridiculously cheap products made in, guess where, China. Garages and bedroom closets are packed to the gills with unopened boxes of "must-haves" purchased from Amazon, QVC, Home Shopping Network and retailers from coast-to-coast. Sure, I know, it sounded good at the time. It razzled and dazzled your senses; it was a delight to your eyes, so you dug out your Visa or MasterCard and picked up the phone. Will we ever learn?

My point here is that we purchase way more stuff than we will ever need. Imagine if we actually purchased only what was necessary. Would we continue to require bigger homes with three-car garages and full-sized basements and attics just to hold all the stuff we bought, used, and became tired of before we actually used it up – or used it at all?

Recently I had a client who asked me to help her prepare her home for sale. Before we could begin staging we would have to downsize the contents of her closets and drawers. That might not sound like a big deal, but her closet was 10' wide and 20' long. I could barely see the carpet. Initially her homework was to go through her massive collection of bras and underwear and select only the ones she wanted to keep. The total bra count when she started was 73. When she finished, it was down to 17.

No judgment here, ladies and fellow bra enthusiasts, but "the girls" do not need 73 of these contraptions! I applauded her for being willing to take such drastic measures to bring her collection to a reasonable number.

You might remember George Carlin's comedic bit called 'Stuff" I think he said it best. Look it up on YouTube sometime. It's hilarious!

A nugget of advice.

Try doing what I did a few years ago and disconnect from your cable service. Subscribe to Netflix, Hulu or another movie provider and only watch the programs you love.

Commercial-free public television is also a wonderful – and educational alternative. Not only will you stop spending money on manipulative commercial television, but you'll probably sleep better and spend less!

The furry sandwich

One day my assistant and I went to visit our old friend Mary at her new apartment. Today just happened to be both my and Mary's birthdays. Our plan was to take Mary a fuzzy little stuffed Yorkie dog she desperately wanted me to retrieve from her home along with a birthday card. She was thrilled! In her little girl voice, Mary cooed and cajoled her little stuffed pet. It was good to see her again and I could tell she appreciated the company as well as the gift.

We had relocated her awhile back and had set up the apartment to suit her taste. The only thing missing was all the extraneous clutter she'd become accustomed to at her house. Now, she could easily motor through doorways and in to the kitchen without as much as a pause. She was safe, at least for the time being. Evidenced by the growing piles of papers on every surface in the apartment, I had a sneaking suspicion Mary was falling back in to her old habits. I knew it wouldn't be long before I'd be called back to bail her out.

We chatted away catching up on all the latest news, and as my hand rested on the handle to the refrigerator door I could not resist convincing her to let me take a look inside. She gave me one of her signature giggles and confessed to harboring large quantities of chocolates.

Sure enough, there were boxes and BOXES of chocolates, and some looked scarily familiar from 10 months ago when we moved her there. You know that look – all crusty with a white film overtop? My mind raced back to the 30-year old ham and I looked at Mary with a knowing eye. She knew she had been caught.

I became curious when I saw a dozen or so black Styrofoam take-out containers jammed in the door and on every shelf. Assuming some level of earned authority over Mary's situation I began opening the containers. It was déjà vu! My assistant grabbed a giant garbage bag and held it open wide while I reluctantly peered inside each container chucking box after box in the trash. Yuck!

Mary just giggled.

My assistant's eyes became big as saucers and I just shook my head, smiled and worked my way through the mess. Old cookies, pies, fruits, breads and such made their way in to the trash.

The last time I'd taken a picture at Mary's was of the infamous ham. As I think back I wish I had mounted the ham on a nice wooden base with an engraved brass plate and given it to some quirky museum that featured oddities of human hoarding. After all, it was an antique of sorts.

Mary was holding true to form because inside one black Styrofoam container was the greenest, fuzziest most perfect sandwich I had ever seen. I told my assistant we were assuming possession of the sandwich so I could take a picture for our very own Hall of Shame. Mary giggled, and gave her new stuffed dog a squeeze. It was a precious moment.

Gold, guns & garbage

Whenever I give a talk to a group of retirees or seniors there is always a grouping of favorite stories I tell to illustrate some key points. One of my favorite stories is when I was hired to process a very large old home in Philadelphia. The family was of some importance, so when it was time to relocate the matriarch to a smaller home they first attempted to protect their privacy by handling the project themselves. Three years went by and the family had worked hard to get rid of things and clean out the house. That's when I got the call. On the other end of the line was Jennifer, one of the daughters. She asked if I could come for a consultation. Now I love homes like this, not to own or live in, but to process. Most often the people have lived there for more than 40 or 50 years and have never gotten rid of anything. It is truly a treasure cultivator's dream.

Once the family decided to enlist our services we set forth to begin work on the home. There were eight bedrooms, four bathrooms, huge living spaces, multiple porches and an attic. Jennifer and I walked through the house and talked about what had already been done and what still needed attention.

In the center of one of the smaller upstairs bedrooms was a huge pile of trash. The edges all around the room were clear with no furniture remaining. So, I asked her about the pile and she confirmed that it was all trash and gave me permission to bag it and toss it out.

She needed a break so she left for lunch. Call it intuition, curiosity or whatever you like, but I grabbed a large trash bag and set to work on the pile. For good reason I have learned not to trust other people's definition of a trash pile. As I worked through the items I discovered some lovely old portraits and an oval pewter tray filled with watches, jewelry and other trinkets.

"Surely, they didn't mean to throw these things away." I said to myself.

So, I set them aside. A few minutes later I noticed several very small white envelopes with family members' names neatly written on front. I lightly shook one. It wasn't empty. I turned it over in my hand and out dropped small gold coins. Each and every envelope contained gold.

"SURELY, they didn't intend to throw this away!"

So, I set them aside and finished putting the trash in the bag. I waited for Jennifer to return from lunch. Before we stopped for our break I asked her if I could show her some items I had found – just to be sure they *meant* to throw them away. Of course, I knew better, but when people grow weary of the process and get careless they miss things. It happens all the time.

Jennifer sat down and I proceeded to show her my discoveries. She was ecstatic about the portraits and old photos and was happy to have them back. I said, "If you liked that, I think you'll like this too." I showed her the oval tray filled with watches and silver coins. Her expression was one of complete disbelief as she asked, "Where did you find these?" I replied, "I found them in the trash pile up in the bedroom." I had her attention but knew the real discovery was about to be unveiled.

Again, I said, "Well, if you liked that, surely you'll like this." I asked her to open her hand and placed the gold coins and envelopes into her hand. She shrieked! "Where did you find these?" "In the pile of trash," I replied. Remember what I said before about being able to trust the person you hire?

More than once while processing a home I have found guns and ammunition. This is a very touchy subject on a number of levels. There have been many cases where I discover a gun or guns in the home and the client, often a widow, simply wants them gone. This takes extra special handling as guns are often mistakenly left loaded. In these cases, it is simply best to call in a registered, licensed FFL gun dealer or expert to assess the guns. Once they've been evaluated, guns and ammunition can be sold via legal channels, through qualified auction houses or disposed of through the police department.

When it comes to guns, if you don't know what you're doing, DO NOT HANDLE THEM!

Now for some trash talk.

I have seen my share of trash. It is always the first step in clearing a home so you can see what lies beneath the piles. It is the quickest way to gain clarity before sorting for auction and donation. Often the client doesn't even know what they have. Once clear of the trash she can then decide whether or not she wants to keep the items or let them go.

One of my most heart-wrenching cases ever was Jim. He suffered a leg amputation from the knee down and was confined to a wheelchair on the first floor of his two-story home. His wife had recently passed quite unexpectedly from an aneurism and he was no longer able to remain in his home.

The living room, kitchen and family room were fairly livable. Jim had to sleep in the family room and hadn't been upstairs for almost five years. Come to find out, Jim's wife had been suffering from depression. Their two grown children lived out-of-state and hadn't visited in quite some time.

With Jim's permission, I ventured upstairs to assess the situation. I can't begin to tell you how bad it was, and worse yet, Jim had no earthly idea of its condition. Not only were the floors not visible, but the master bedroom was an unspeakable disaster. There was money, jewelry and clothing strewn on the floor, across the dressers and bed. It looked as though it had been ransacked. The hallway to the bathroom was impassible. It was one of the saddest things I had ever seen and I was the one who would have to explain to Jim what to expect.

So, I took pictures of each room and went downstairs to show him. I knew he would be crushed, but I didn't have any choice. I was right. He sat there in his wheelchair with his face buried in his hands, and cried. My heart broke for him.

I offered to leave the master bedroom off limits until he felt comfortable allowing me in to take care of the room. In the meantime, we focused on the rest of the house and made the upstairs look nice for potential showings. The attic, main floor and basement would also have to be processed.

It was quite some time before Jim finally acquiesced and agreed to let me address the master bedroom. This, my friends, is how you learn to be ultra-sensitive. Each day I would bring items to him for review. We found buckets of coins throughout the house and each day would place them in front of him like a gift offering.

One day in particular I came across a huge bucket of silver coins. All this time he had been giving the coins to his neighbor to take to the coin machine at the bank. While this was fine for everyday coins, I advised him that this batch should be handled very differently. He agreed and I met with my coin dealer who offered a considerable amount for the lot. Jim was very happy with the outcome, and I think he learned a valuable lesson in the process.

Let's return to the master bedroom for a moment. Fortunately, we were able to donate his wife's beautiful clothes, costume jewelry, shoes and handbags to Wings for Success – a women's organization that helps dress ladies who are trying to re-enter the workforce and can't afford to purchase nice clothes for interviews.

I sorted through her jewelry, checked with Jim, then sold whatever he didn't want to keep or pass on to his daughter. All that remained was either sold at auction or to private buyers. When all was said and done Jim's home was ready to put on the market and he was able to bring closure to a very painful phase of his life.

I love telling this story.

One of my favorite memories of all times is the accounting of a true treasure hunt. I was hired by a client's son to handle a major clean-up project at their family home. Since the rest of the family lived out-of-state they weren't able to dedicate the time needed to put their father's home in order – the job was simply too overwhelming and would require an enormous amount of time and effort. Their primary concern was for his overall living conditions.

Bill, a spry and energetic 92-year-old was still driving, managing his own finances, traveling and keeping up with world affairs. His positive attitude and sense of adventure helped make him one of my most interesting and enjoyable clients of all.

Bill had lived in the same home for over 60 years, his wife had long-since passed and the house had evolved into a completely disastrous condition. From basement to attic, four floors high, was evidence of Bill's inability to keep up with the on-going need to even keep the house clean. As much as he tried, it was simply too much for him to handle. Understandably, the family wanted to honor their father's wish to remain in his own home for as long as possible. But, in order for that to happen they needed someone like me to create a clean, orderly, safe and manageable environment.

As with most older people, Bill had accumulated massive amounts of paper. Every nook and cranny harbored pile after pile of old tax records, article clippings, receipts and magazines. Bookshelves, almost too many to count, were stacked with hard-backs of virtually every genre, evidencing his myriad interests.

Our daily conversations were both interesting and revealing. When you've lived for over 90 years there's much to share – that is, if they're willing to talk – and if you're willing to listen. This is one of the reasons I love working with seniors. Due to the nature of my work I spend a lot of time in conversation with my clients. Sometimes I feel sad for the families who live far away or for those who are simply not interested in getting to know their parent as an adult.

Periodically throughout my time with Bill he would casually mention to me that many years ago he'd buried some coins in his yard. For the longest time I acknowledged his memory of the treasure and continued to move throughout the house putting things in order. Finally, after I had heard the story enough times, I decided to come prepared to help Bill unearth his treasure. It would have been easier if he'd remembered exactly where it was buried! "It's under one of the front windows." he recanted, but couldn't remember for sure. So, I with shovel in hand, and Bill comfortably seated on the front porch, began to dig. One foot down, then two, three feet...I asked, "Bill, how far down did you bury the money?" He couldn't remember. "Exactly what kind of container did you put the coins in?" As best he could, he described some plastic tubes – a couple of them. I still didn't have an accurate visual impression of the containers, their size or their contents.

Being a tenacious person – I kept digging. There I stood in a four-foot by two-foot-deep hole, rubber boots and all, covered in mud. Once again, I asked Bill if he was certain about the location. Luckily, a trip to the basement would help solve the mystery. Lo and behold, there was a rusted-out safe, sitting in a shallow pool of water. As best he could recall there might actually be a treasure map inside however, he didn't remember the combination to the safe! For the next two hours Bill and I pried, dismantled and pretty much beat the crap out of the safe, and finally the door popped open. Not only did we find the map, but a smelly, moldy and indiscernible collection of old papers and documents. We were ecstatic! I couldn't believe my eyes...there was actually a real treasure map he had drawn over 50 years ago. The bad news was that all this time I'd been digging under the wrong window!

With a quick lunch to rejuvenate my body and my spirits, I dawned my muddy rubber boots and started digging under window number two. Since the house was set way back from the street and was overgrown by trees and underbrush, passers-by weren't likely to see what we were up to. An hour or so went by and there was still no sign of the tubes. I was beginning to think he'd perhaps forgotten that he'd already dug them up. I kept asking him questions like, "How far down had he buried them? What exactly had he buried? Had he ever told anyone about the coins?" I was a little dismayed when he told me no one but he knew they existed. Since it was likely the house would ultimately be torn down someday, I was concerned some worker would find the money and the family would be none the wiser. We'll revisit this important aspect of the situation in a minute.

Sure enough, about four feet down, I hit concrete, but according to Bill, he hadn't poured concrete over the tubes. It's a good thing I don't give up easily, because under the concrete slabs were two PVC tubes. It took every ounce of strength I could muster to lift and wedge the tubes to an upright position and hoist them out of the hole. We spread out a tarp and I unscrewed one of the lids. Thousands of silver dimes came pouring out of the tubes! Bill and I rejoiced at having found the once buried, but not forgotten, treasure he had been telling me about for weeks.

Once we'd recovered all of the bounty, we called one of his sons to tell him the story, and of course, he was delighted. About a year-and-a-half passed before Bill cashed in all the dimes – walking away with a check for nearly $12,000! To this day, Bill and I meet for dinner every so often and reminisce about digging up his buried treasure. This is just another reason I love what I do!

Intellectual property heist

Another consultation with a prospective client led me to Beverly, a lovely woman probably close to my age, with beautiful long blonde hair cascading down past her waist. She requested a consultation based on a recommendation by a close friend and colleague. My friend became acquainted with Beverly when she came to her shop in search of a buyer for her recently deceased mother's vintage jewelry and clothing. My friend agreed to visit her mother's home to view the things Beverly wanted to sell and took one look at the house and recommended she call me for help.

There I was, sitting in the living room awaiting the grand tour. She explained to me that one of her brothers was planning to renovate the family home then make it his primary residence. When Beverly was challenged with cleaning out the home on behalf of her mother's estate it became apparent she needed assistance, a lot of it. She had already invested a great deal of her own time and energy but remained bogged down, overwhelmed and depressed. The daunting task of single-handedly processing the entire home had caught up with her.

She armed herself with information gleaned from meetings with numerous experts from area auction houses, charities, cleaning services and the like. Beverly realized she would have to become the general contractor responsible for contacting, interviewing, scheduling, comparison shopping, making decisions *and* doing most of the tedious work herself. None of her three brothers were either willing to accept the lead role in the process, or did they have plans to reimburse Beverly for her time.

One of the biggest mistakes I see families make in the processing of a parent's or relative's home is they fail to establish a fair value for their time. Just because they happen not to be working or are the closest living relative does not mean they should accept responsibility for all the work, or to process the home without some form of compensation. It is a gargantuan task, one for which they will all most certainly be harshly and unfairly criticized for in the end.

If the one in charge of the process is a working adult with a full-time job, family, a home to take care of and her own busy life to tend to, her time is likely scarce. People are busy and the family member with the most flexibility or geographic convenience generally ends up with the lion's share of the responsibility.

This is a bad strategy.

This tactic ultimately breeds resentment that leads to strained relationships between family members. I know because I've been there.

Naturally, I shared with Beverly some key insights into efficiently processing and redirecting the houseful of personal property. Many lovely antiques would need to be taken to a reputable auction house and much could be donated to charities. I told her that if we were to do the job we would collect and take scrap metals to the recycling yard. She would be assured of a level of efficiency and sensitivity justifying the expense the family would likely incur.

Most people don't know with any certainty whether or not they have property worth taking to auction. It takes a skilled and experienced professional who has taken time to stay abreast of market trends to ensure the client that nothing important is missed in the process. It didn't take me long to see that Beverly was simply fishing for enough information to try to tackle the job herself.

Don't get me wrong, I don't mind helping people work through their challenges, and if I sense they can't afford to have someone do it for them, I am always happy to make suggestions and provide contact information and resources. I never heard from Beverly again, but did hear from others in my field that she had taken advantage of numerous people's time in order to educate herself – and then didn't hire anyone – or offer to compensate them for their time. Not cool.

Just a thought.

The longer I do this work the more clearly I see how people become easily attached to their things. A Chippendale desk where a beloved grandmother sat, a red-and-white striped dress the client's mother wore every Fourth of July, a crystal vase that held a fresh bouquet of flowers every Mother's Day – all are vivid reminders of who we are, where we've been and the relationships we've formed with the people in our lives.

When it comes to memories, we're people whose lives are purposed and validated by the things around us. Essentially, they may be meaningless to others, yet in our minds and hearts they've become invaluable.

These are the thoughts and feelings that tend to cause great anxiety when it comes time to let go of all the stuff we've accumulated along the way.

The truth about collectibles

When I think of the incredible variety of objects my clients have collected, I am amazed and sometimes dumbfounded. From closets full of linens to worthless online purchases, they've collected and hoarded mountains of both valuable and worthless things. For the most part I believe people don't intentionally set out to be excessive in their buying habits however, as time goes on what started out as an innocent desire for a beautiful object or collection became evidence of excessive consumption.

For a time, my particular fetish was anything to do with frogs. Once my friends and family caught on, my collection grew. Before I knew it, I had frogs everywhere! For some it's trains, art supplies, fabric, shoes, handbags, perfume bottles, dolls, bras, decorative plates or complete sets of dishes.

In a former phase of my life I was a senior writer for the Franklin Mint. It was my job to write creative copy designed to entice people to buy what we were selling. I loved working there and thoroughly enjoyed my job. Many of the products we sold such as the dolls, chess sets and porcelain objects were very well made. As a copywriter, my goal was to get people to collect an entire series of plates, pocket knives and the like. Prior to the Internet the public was not privy to how much of this stuff was out there and as a result perceived their value to be much greater than they actually were.

Oftentimes my clients were disappointed to learn that their collection of FM plates would have a resale value of about $1.00 each. Ultimately, I believe the downfall of The Franklin Mint was largely due to the pressure of immense competition from the Internet. It probably sounds terrible to say but I used to get paid to convince people to buy things they didn't really need, couldn't afford, and didn't have a place for...and now they would be paying me to get rid of it for them. Ouch! Sorry.

One of my clients, a single woman in her late 50s had a thing for china. While helping her downsize prior to her move, I counted eight complete sets of high-end china. Bear in mind, she lived alone and rarely entertained. After much consternation I was able to talk her down to keeping all but five sets.

It can be difficult for the average person to know what is worth collecting and what is ultimately going to be worthless. When I was a little girl I had one of the largest collections of Wrigley's chewing gum wrappers you have ever seen. I meticulously sorted and banded them together according to flavor; Juicy Fruit, Spearmint and Doublemint. During one of our many moves my precious collection mysteriously disappeared. For that I blame my mother. Needless to say, it was not a particularly valuable collection.

What amazes me is the ungodly amount of money people will spend on trendy things such as Beanie Babies. Since starting this business back in 2005, I have handled literally thousands of the little darlings. Back in the heyday people swarmed to stores paying top dollar for colorful cute bean-stuffed animals of every kind. Some were even selling online for hundreds of dollars.

Most recently I had a client with a collection of over 600 Beanie Babies, all were clean and stored thoughtfully in plastic bins. We sorted them by character, counted each one, researched them and ultimately bagged them for donation.

Bear in mind, whenever I am responsible for assessing a collection of any kind, I always research the item or items thoroughly. I cannot begin to tell you how many hours I have spent sorting Beanie Babies – checking tags, looking for specific colors, and diligently trying to find the valuable ones in the batch. Honestly, I can tell you I have never once found even one worth more than its tag value.

Historically my clients have allowed me to donate their Beanie Baby collections. We used to hand them out during Holiday House each year, but never managed to give them all away. So, one year I teamed up with a teacher from an area elementary school. She was so excited about the massive gift that she came up with a creative learning project for her class. The assignment was to make a business of selling the Beanie Babies and then donate the proceeds to a local charity.

The kids were responsible for developing a website, they wrote jingles, made signs and did morning announcements over the PA system. Their plan was to hold a three-day sale at the school and let kids buy the Beanies for $1.00 - $1.25 each. Within the first two days they sold out and the children had successfully raised over $600 for charity. Not bad for a bunch of seven and eight-year-olds!

When the project was over I was asked to speak to the class and was amazed at their enthusiasm and dedication to the project. The teacher creatively turned the generous donation from one of my clients in to a major success story for her class. My client was thrilled that her mother's collection had made such a tremendous impact on so many levels. All these years later I still collect and donate to the school all of the Beanie Babies I come across. Now, the program has become an annual event. The point is that there are many opportunities to creatively redirect some kinds of collections and perhaps take a nice tax write-off in the process.

It seems every client has collected one thing or another that must be dealt with. Part of my job is to ensure we're making intelligent recommendations on their behalf. I often tell them I am the voice of reason, and when it comes to perceived valuables I may end up being the bearer of bad news. What some think is valuable is often not, and what is mistakenly assumed to be trash can actually be treasure.

My best advice is before throwing anything away is to ask an expert. Take photographs of valuables, send them off to reputable agents, research online to see if anyone has sold the same item and for how much. If someone is unfamiliar with eBay, absolute auctions or with a computer in general, he should seriously consult with experts.

If it is deemed that selling via auction is the best avenue, it is wise to consider timing. As with any business the auction market fluctuates. There are better times of the year to sell at auction, and depending on the merchandise some items sell better by season. Consider the possible return on a nice snow blower in October versus June – or a patio set in May instead of December.

When it comes to the auction alternative to selling goods, there are many important factors to keep in mind. For example, in my business I deal with more than a half-dozen different auction houses. Because I come across such a wide variety of merchandise, I am responsible to select the auction or auctions I feel are the most appropriate. They all have strengths and weaknesses, or rather specialties.

Some high-end auctions will not accept an item valued to sell for less than $5,000 and for others the low-end limit may be $1,000. If the majority of items are considered "common," then I am likely to take them where there are no minimums – this is referred to as "absolute auction." Be aware that in the auction business - one size does not fit all.

There are also auctions that specialize in high-end collectibles such as slot machines, guns, cash registers, dolls, money, marbles, jewelry, militaria, sports memorabilia, fine art and such. Others are more geared to liquidating complete contents of retail stores of all kinds. So, it's important to know and understand what their specialty is.

Some clients may wish to consider a buy-out or on-site estate sale. Either of these might be fine depending upon the situation; however, be aware there are some unscrupulous people out there looking to take advantage of unsuspecting clients.

One quick story is an example of what I mean. While processing some items for a client I came across an old doll house. It was in decent condition. I asked the owner what her perception of its value was, for which she replied, "Oh, it's really quite nice. I suppose around $300 or so." While researching the doll house, I discovered it was made by "Bliss." Just so happens one of the auction houses I deal with on a regular basis was highlighted in the book I had been using for reference. Before taking my client's property to that auction I already had a good idea of its' potential value. My client was thrilled when her dollhouse sold at auction for $1,700.

My point here is to illustrate the notion that had I not been a reputable representative for my client I might have offered to purchase the house from her for $300. Likely she would have been very happy with that, and I would have been happy too...and $1,400 richer. I'm just saying...seller, beware.

You think you can do this?

When I'm sharing seemingly countless stories of my journey while building this business, people often remark, "I would love to do what you do!" or "I'm really good at organizing and getting rid of stuff." I'm not sure that my knowing smile conveys the depth and breadth of what it takes to do this kind of work on a regular basis, because it is so much more than just organizing, throwing away things, crawling in attics, basements, barns and sheds.

There is virtually no way to short cut the learning curve to gaining product knowledge or understanding human nature. By this I mean that unless a person has been involved in the antiques or auction business on some level, he or she is simply not qualified to intelligently process a home containing items that should be sold rather than donated or thrown away. Properly processing a house is grueling, messy and sometimes dangerous work that invariably comes with the monumental responsibility of earning and maintaining the client's trust. Unfortunately, there are some people in the business who wouldn't think of telling a client they had found something of great value while processing their home.

"Finders keepers!" Right? Wrong.

As professionals in the business it is our responsibility to protect our client's interests, whether they realize they have something of value or not. If you or someone you know is interested in forming a business similar to mine, you might want to offer a day or two of your time to shadow a professional in your area. I guarantee, after a couple of days dealing with the challenges of de-cluttering, organizing or staging someone else's home, it's likely you'll view your own home as never before. The stark realization of how easily things can become unmanageable will change the way you think about being a consumer of meaningless goods.

One thing is for sure – at a point in time in every person's life, she will be faced with multiple transitions that ultimately lead to the complete re-direction of virtually everything she owns. Most likely her stuff will end up in one of two places: in someone else's home or at the dump. So, everyone should be careful about how they spend their money, about what they choose to collect, and how much importance they place on what they own.

NEWS FLASH!

It's all JUST STUFF.

Ultimately, you can't take it with you!

5-Prong Evaluation Process & 22 Questions You Should Ask Yourself

When deciding what you can do to move toward a simpler, more organized lifestyle, I recommend you place all of your belongings into one of five categories outlined in my 5-PRONG DECISION MAKING PROCESS.

1. What you want to keep
2. What you can give away or sell to family and friends
3. What can be sold via private sale, auction, online sale or consignment
4. What can be donated to charity
5. What should be thrown away

Then ask yourself the following questions:

1. **Do you need or love all the stuff you've collected and stored away for the future?**

Think about redirecting things you're tired of looking at or have been storing in the basement, attic or garage for more than 2 years. Have things gotten out of control? Do you or anyone else even care about these things anymore?

2. When you're gone who will want your possessions?

Are your grown children going to want your things, or do they already have homes full of their own stuff? Do they care about old photos, hand-me-downs, mementos or historical genetic records? Really, ask them! You might be surprised at their answer.

3. Do your possessions have monetary value?

If you have reason to believe your things have value, consider having a fair market valuation performed by an experienced appraiser. Be willing to do some preliminary research online before getting rid of a prized possession. If you can sell some things yourself you can avoid paying a commission. This tends to be way more work than people think, so be sure you understand the time commitment and relative cost.

4. How will you get rid of all the stuff no one in the family wants?

Aside from selling personal property privately or at auction, there's also consignment shops, online sales, or even a yard sale. Consider donating to your favorite charity, church, library, or a local school to see if they can use anything you no longer need. Do a little research and be sure to get a donation receipt for your files. All of these options come with pros and cons.

5. Are you living a simple, uncluttered life?

Take a look at your surroundings. Think about how you might redesign your home to suit the current phase of your life. Do you love your stuff or are you tired of it? Is all the stuff oppressing you and tying you to the past? Do you feel bogged down and overwhelmed?

6. When was the last time you went through your closets, cupboards, attic, basement and garage, and got rid of all the unnecessary junk?

Try rotating from room-to-room on a regular basis. Continue paring down supplies, clothing, tools and other stuff you no longer want or need. Categorize everything so you know what you have. Having supplies spread throughout your home may be confusing your ability to remember what you need to purchase.

7. Do you know how to properly dispose of hazardous materials?

Check with your township or city for instructions and collection dates. Anything that may be considered hazardous to the environment needs to be disposed of properly. Electronic equipment can no longer go in your trash. Some big box stores such as Best Buy offer recycling services for small electronics and such. Use up all the pesticides, oil, cleaning products and such before you move.

8. Are you planning to sell your home?

If so, think about investing in a seller's home inspection so you'll have a good idea what remedies potential buyers are likely to negotiate. Decide which things you are willing to proactively correct or improve. Obtain estimates from no fewer than 2-3 contractors then prioritize a list of improvements based upon where you're likely to get the most bang for the buck when you sell. This will position you to properly negotiate your selling price. If your property is not in line with the current market rates and you're not willing to make improvements, be prepared to accept a lower selling price.
CAUTION - Once you've been made aware of an issue you're obligated to disclose that information when you list your home for sale. That said, some people prefer to take their chances with the buyer's inspection instead.

9. In preparation for selling your home, would you benefit from having it professionally staged?

If you have a knack for decorating and the ability to be totally objective, then you might want to try this yourself. If not, then I highly recommend asking your realtor to recommend a professional stager. You must know your target market and then update the look and feel of the home as best you can.

Consider basic staging vs. mid-range vs. high-end staging complete with significant improvements as part of your strategy. In almost every case staging is an investment that's well-worth the money.

One thing is for sure...

...you won't get a second chance to make a first impression!

10. **Evaluate your home objectively. Begin the process at the end of the driveway. Make note of anything a potential buyer might find objectionable.**
    Here are some of the questions you should answer as you progress from the outside to the inside of the property:
    a. Is the yard and landscaping well-groomed and maintained?
    b. How does the roof look? When was the last time it was replaced? Have the gutters been cleaned lately?
    c. What is the condition of the siding, decks, pool and garage? Does it need to be power washed?
    d. Does it need to be painted, the stucco repaired or the decks sanded and re-stained?
    e. Then start at the front door and walk through the house as though you were a potential buyer. Take time to look carefully at the walls, doors, floors, the kitchen, bathrooms, basement and attic.
    f. What is the condition and cleanliness of the house? Is it well-maintained? What message does it send?

g. Check for clutter. If there are piles of papers, magazines, clothing, trash, dog or cat hair, pet food, cat boxes, tons of collectibles, stuff on top of counters and in corners – then get ready to get busy. You might not mind how it looks but trust me, potential buyers will notice everything! Be honest with yourself. Buyers will be brutal in their assessment, so be prepared, because they're looking for any reason to offer you less than you're asking.

11. Are family members willing and able to assist you in making improvements?

People usually mean well when they offer to help however, when the time comes – their schedule often doesn't permit, or they simply don't want to do the work after all. Be realistic in your expectations.

12. Are you inhibited by any physical or cognitive health issues that would preclude you from doing the work yourself?

If you are unable to lift, move, bend or reach due to physical constraints, I recommend you hire someone to help you. This is a very physical process and you have to be realistic. Ask yourself the question, "If I can do this myself, why haven't I already done it?" Don't hurt yourself! It's just not worth it.

13. Are you familiar with area auction houses, re-sale consignment shops and online services?

If not, ask your friends, your attorney, realtor, financial planner, doctor or church official who they would recommend. It's likely some of the same names will keep popping up. Request an in-home consultation in order to find someone you feel confident to handle the job.

14. Do you know which charities accept household goods versus furniture, food, pet supplies, etc.?

Not all charities can or will pick up furniture – some don't accept clothing. Many charities won't enter your home or move furniture from inside your house and can only pick up items that have been prepared, boxed and placed outside or in the garage. Be sure to do a little research online so you know which charities are willing to pick up from your home. Some will ask you to take digital photographs so they can see if the items will be appropriate for their shop.
I happen to be a big fan of Vietnam Veterans Association, Purple Heart, Green Drop, Habitat for Humanity, and other smaller area charities and church compassion programs that give things away rather than charge for them.

15. Are you able to transport donated items yourself?

If there is a local GreenDrop, Goodwill, Salvation Army, SPCA or other drop site in your neighborhood, decide if you can get things there by yourself. Be sure you know what the hours and days of operation are before you cart the stuff over, or go online and arrange for a pick-up of your donations.

16. Are you aware of guidelines for shredding important documents?

Check to see if there is a professional shredding service in your area. Some of them will pick up and shred on location. Some area senior homes, banks and businesses host shredding events throughout the year. Don't make it easy for identity thieves. Shred anything with account numbers, social security numbers, vital statistics and other personal information that could potentially compromise your privacy. Keep old tax returns only as long as is required by law. No need to retain and store decades of returns. They serve no purpose and take up valuable space.

17. Do you know how long to keep important documents?

Some documents should be retained for life and others can be disposed of after an account, item or property has been sold. Ask your attorney for guidance – or look it up on the Internet.

18. Do you know a group of professionals you can call for advice?

Consult with your attorney, financial planner, realtor, church officials and friends for referrals. You might be surprised to know how many others have been through the same process and are familiar with knowledgeable and reputable professionals in your area.

19. Can you imagine living a simpler, less cluttered lifestyle?

Envision your home without all the clutter. Look at your home environment – does it make you feel frustrated, angry, hemmed-in, oppressed or overwhelmed? If so, it's time to take action! Imagine the weight of the world off your shoulders and give yourself permission to make a fresh start. Don't be afraid – be proactive. Don't wait until your choices are limited due to declining health, divorce or even a death in the family.

20. Can you stop yourself from buying more stuff?

Be honest...is there some void in your life you've been trying to fill with more clothes, shoes, cars, groceries or whatever it is you tend to buy? Trust me, it only makes things worse. Instant gratification never lasts long and about the time the credit card bills arrive, buyer's remorse sets in. If you've made up your mind and want to make some lasting changes, start by going on a buying fast. Commit to stay out of your favorite stores for at least a month. First, organize and review what you have, then carefully evaluate what you really NEED.

21. It's quite likely a bit of trash will be generated during the process of downsizing. Are you familiar with

alternative ways of disposing of large quantities of trash?

Consider calling a local junk removal company to haul away excess trash or request a 20 or 30-yard dumpster. The cost of a unit will depend upon the weight of the load along with drop fees. A junk hauler can make this a much easier process.

22. **How long did it take your home to arrive in its current condition? And, how much do you expect it to cost to remedy the situation?**

It's easy to underestimate or undervalue the cost, time and energy it will require to regain control over the mess. It may have taken decades for it to get that way and it's highly unlikely even a professional can work a miracle overnight.
Remember, the professional strategist is there to solve your problem. She is your advocate and she's there to protect your interests and attain the goals set forth. Communication during the process is key. Don't hesitate to ask for financial updates as the project progresses.

Ready to take action?

There's no time like the present. Continuing to put it off will only make things worse. Whatever you do, don't leave the daunting task of clearing your home to your children. It's an unfair burden that may well be met with added emotional distress, work, and resentment.

Trust me on this – family and friends don't usually have the time, experience or insight required to effectively process your home. If you want a say in the way it's handled – don't procrastinate – be proactive and do this while you're able to make your own choices. It's one of the greatest gifts you can give your children.

If you <u>need</u> help – get help!

If the condition of your home poses a greater challenge than simply getting organized, I suggest you seek out a reputable lifestyle transition specialist. Based on your particular goals and objectives a true professional will strategize and efficiently orchestrate the entire process for you. She will most certainly save you valuable time, money and, most of all... your sanity.

Consider contacting the National Association of Productivity and Organizing (NAPO). Their database will help to identify someone in your area with the skillsets that match your needs.

NAPO
856.380.6828
https://www.NAPO.net

Life goes on

I recently moved from this sweet little house my son, mother and I had lived in for many years. I loved that home and leaving it was indeed way more traumatic than I'd anticipated. Bear in mind...for over a decade I'd been responsible for more than 1,000 moves for other people, and am regarded as a highly-experienced professional in my field. It's important to understand, even those of us who do this for a living aren't exempt from the deep emotional feelings associated with letting go of the past. I too had to objectively evaluate everything I'd amassed over the years. Some of it was easy – some way more difficult. The sheer volume of my belongings was a bit overwhelming. And I'm not even a pack-rat!

Even though the next phase of my personal life was moving forward in a wonderful and welcome way, I was saddened by the reality of finally letting go. It's where I'd raised my son, who has since graduated college, launched his career and moved away. The pleasure and privilege of my mother's company for so many of those years had also come to an end as she moved out west to share a home with my sister. Thankfully, I was able to redirect much of my excess to my immediate family.

My point is when it comes to the subject of downsizing, staging, moving or cleaning out, it's often a much bigger job than we expect. It's seemingly easier to avoid those areas of our lives that harbor our memories – both good and bad. It can be really hard to let go of stuff that has helped define us and our past. After all, it's our personal history, and up until now, it's "where we've been," not "where we're headed." Sometimes the unknown that lies ahead is scarier than the certainty of the past. But, we shouldn't be afraid – because the end result will be liberating.

Now that I've crossed over to my next new and exciting phase of life, I almost never think of my little house -that was until my son texted me a picture he had taken of us on the front porch our last day there. I got choked up, swallowed hard and was grateful I'd survived the move.

Life goes on – and guess what?

I don't miss anything I let go of!

In closing

As with any profession there are experts and there are hacks. The old adage, "You get what you pay for" is usually right. At any rate, it is never easy to undo what can take a lifetime to create. During every phase of life, we tend to acquire things that represent where we are in our life path. When we are starting out we buy things to make us more comfortable in our homes; then we start having children and buy bigger homes – and that invokes an entirely new set of needs. When our children grow up and leave we no longer require all that space or the mountains of stuff we've saved over the years. Finally, we're now free to liberate ourselves from the oppressive accumulation of decades gone by.

Simplifying your lifestyle should start with your personal surroundings. If you make a conscious decision to, you *can* live more simply. I encourage you to consider how much more fun you could be having, or how much more you could travel or even have time to learn a new skill or language - if you weren't bogged down with so much stuff.

I am a huge proponent of lightening your load. I highly recommend you not buy-in to all the sales gimmicks out there, and for goodness sake don't sit comatose in front of television watching infomercials and then buy all the stuff they're trying to sell you. Remember, their goal is to get you to buy the stuff from them so they don't have it in their inventory! Seriously, buy only what you truly need. Decide what's important and whether or not you should spend your money in excess. It's the people in your life who are special – not the stuff.

I hope you have enjoyed reading some of the fun and interesting accounts of my journey while dealing with other people's stuff. I have gained a wealth of knowledge from all of these experiences and in certain situations have been able to envision myself in myriad possible life scenarios. That experience has virtually scared me straight! For most people all it takes is seeing how other people end up and how oppressed they are by excess consumption and inaction. The good news is – it's never too late to break-out of your old habits and make positive changes that can last the rest of your life.

How you choose to live is very personal and I respect everyone's right to do so. Your home is your castle and you can life as you like. When it comes to your stuff, I want you to remember two things: whether it is worthless or valuable, it's still just stuff – and you can't take it with you. "Things" are only worth what someone else is willing to pay. So, don't get caught up in your perception of value.

Thanks to all of my clients for this incredible journey.

SPECIAL THANKS

When I decided to write this book, I drew inspiration from hundreds of clients I've served over the years. Along the way I've picked up bits and pieces of insight through interactions with individuals and families that I felt were important enough to share with others. And now my hope is that what I learned will help others gain the knowledge and understanding needed so they don't repeat some of the same mistakes.

Three people have been particularly supportive throughout this entire effort: my mother, my son and my sister. For years they have endured my ravenous passion for excellence and my high tolerance for risk. Until recently, my mother worked side-by-side with me from the beginning. She has always been a tireless and dedicated woman whose strength and determination were second to none. My son stood by me through thick and thin as I spent 60 to 80 hours a week striving to earn enough to support the three of us. My lovely and eternally supportive sister always took time to listen to me, as year after year I struggled to grow my business while maintaining some degree of balance in my personal life. These are the people who have most helped me stay grounded and sane.

My experience of writing has been greatly enhanced by my friendship with the well-known best-selling author, Bruce Mowday. I treasure our years of creative brainstorming sessions, shared tables at area events, good food and wine, and most of all his willingness to coach and mentor me. Bruce is my connection to the real world of writing and publishing and I am forever grateful.

And to the special guy in my life whose continued support and encouragement helped me focus my energies on finishing this book. When I found it difficult to stay focused and motivated, or the process became daunting, he became my biggest advocate. His undying love has brought me back home to the deepest parts of my true self. This, I hope, will catapult me in to writing more and better books in the future.

Last but not least, I want to thank God for giving me the courage to follow my dreams. He has blessed me with good friends, a solid family, and the determination to "never give up" – no matter how difficult life becomes. In the midst of "dukkha," God has been there for me.

TESTIMONIALS

Some of Sheree's clients have said it best...

"Sheree's firm transformed the difficult and time-consuming job of distributing a loved one's belongings in to a stress-less and trouble-free event where every items' final disposition, whether for sale, charity or trash, was fully documented."
Eric C. – Paoli, PA

"Sheree and her crew quickly and efficiently helped me decide what to take with me and what could be sold or donated. Each day the excess disappeared! I was delighted. I could finally see the light at the end of the tunnel."
Ann Marie N. – West Chester, PA

"You saved my life! My mental state at the time was such that I really needed rescuing, and there you were. It was truly amazing to deal with someone with such an extraordinary work ethic."
Carole C. – Downingtown, PA

"I would like to thank you for your help in processing my mother's house with intention and sensitivity. Although normally I love big overwhelming jobs, this was a task that had me paralyzed. I offer respect and gratitude for your excellent service."
Eugenie D. – Wilmington, DE

For more information about Richnow LifeStyle Transitions visit our website at www.LifeStyleTransitions.us.

For interviews, to book a speaking engagement or to purchase books in quantity please call or send your request to:

srichnow@LifeStyleTransitions.us
or call 610.558.1250